Catholic Bishops in the United States

Catholic Bishops in the United States

Church Leadership in the Third Millennium

STEPHEN J. FICHTER

THOMAS P. GAUNT, SJ

CATHERINE HOEGEMAN, CSJ

PAUL M. PERL

Fr. Stephen Fichter

OXFORD
UNIVERSITY PRESS

OXFORD
UNIVERSITY PRESS

Oxford University Press is a department of the University of Oxford. It furthers
the University's objective of excellence in research, scholarship, and education
by publishing worldwide. Oxford is a registered trade mark of Oxford University
Press in the UK and certain other countries.

Published in the United States of America by Oxford University Press
198 Madison Avenue, New York, NY 10016, United States of America.

Library of Congress Cataloging-in-Publication Data
Names: Fichter, Stephen J., author.
Title: Catholic Bishops in the United States : church leadership in the
third millennium / Stephen J. Fichter, Thomas P. Gaunt SJ,
Catherine Hoegeman CSJ, Paul M. Perl.
Description: New York : Oxford University Press, 2019. |
Includes bibliographical references and index.
Identifiers: LCCN 2018040317 (print) | LCCN 2018048449 (ebook) |
ISBN 9780190920296 (updf) | ISBN 9780190920302 (epub) |
ISBN 9780190920289 (hardcover) | ISBN 9780190920319 (online content)
Subjects: LCSH: Catholic Church—United States—Bishops. |
Christian leadership—Catholic Church. |
Catholic Church—United States—History—21st century.
Classification: LCC BX1407.B57 (ebook) | LCC BX1407.B57 C38 2019 (print) |
DDC 262/.12273—dc23
LC record available at https://lccn.loc.gov/2018040317

1 3 5 7 9 8 6 4 2

Printed by Sheridan Books, Inc., United States of America

Contents

Foreword

DO YOU REMEMBER how, in response to one of the first questions posed to him as our new Bishop of Rome in 2013, Pope Francis very clearly defined himself first and foremost as a sinner? While this might have shocked many devout Catholics who were expecting him to highlight his role as the Successor of Saint Peter or as the Vicar of Christ, I think that his words resonated deeply within the hearts of bishops throughout the world. I know they resonated in mine.

We bishops are just like everyone else. We are strong and hopeful; we are also weak and sinful. While recognizing the responsibility placed on our shoulders as Successors to the Apostles, and while hoping that all of us are striving to be holy in our own lives, it is clear that we are far from perfect. Speaking of our inadequacies, let me put this out there from the very beginning: We are aware that some of us have lost credibility because of sexual abuse in the Church. For any ways we have not been good shepherds and have disappointed you, we are truly sorry.

If you could walk in our shoes, if you could experience our daily struggles, you would understand why this quote from Saint Augustine (Sermon 340) is one of our favorites:

> Where I'm terrified by what I am for you, I am given comfort by what I am with you. For you I am a bishop, with you, after all, I am a Christian. The first is the name of an office undertaken, the second a name of grace; that one means danger, this one salvation. Finally, as if in the open sea, I am being tossed about by the stormy activity involved in that one; but as I recall by whose blood I have been redeemed, I enter a safe harbor in the tranquil recollection of this one; and thus while toiling away at my own proper office, I take my rest in the marvelous benefit conferred on all of us in common.

Growing up, we never thought we would be wearing these shoes. If you could have seen us as little boys playing ball with our friends, if you could have seen us enter the seminary full of enthusiasm and of fear of the unknown, if you could have been at our first Mass when we trembled for joy, you would know how surprised we are to occupy our episcopal offices today.

And this is why I love this first-ever study of all U.S. Catholic Bishops so much. In these pages you will get to know us bishops (active and retired, Latin Rite and Eastern Rites, ordinaries and auxiliaries) as the real human beings we are. Most Catholics never get to know us beyond the brief contact we have with them at their own Confirmation ceremony or that of a relative or friend. Many people may still have a picture of their Confirmation day from decades ago, but how many can recall the name of the bishop in that old photo? How many of us have had the chance to have a proper sit-down conversation with a bishop? What a powerful juxtaposition it is that we are among the most known and the least known Christians in the world!

I cannot thank Father Stephen Fichter enough for spearheading this project. I recall when he first told me about his idea five years ago. I had just written a commentary for his insightful book *Same Call, Different Men: The Evolution of the Priesthood since Vatican II* that he had written with his colleagues Mary Gautier and Paul Perl from the Center for Applied Research in the Apostolate (CARA). I thought that his idea of dedicating an entire volume to bishops was fantastic then, and I am even more convinced of its value now that I have been able to read the results. Any future study on U.S. bishops will refer to these pages as its baseline.

Initially Father Fichter told me that he thought he could conduct the project by himself, because his original plan was to concentrate only on archbishops as a follow-up study to Father Tom Reese's 1989 book *Archbishop: Inside the Power Structure of the American Catholic Church*. I am very grateful that Cardinal Timothy Dolan, then President of the United States Conference of Catholic Bishops (USCCB), encouraged Father Fichter to expand his project to include all bishops, and not just archbishops. Once the group to be surveyed was thus expanded, he set about building quite an impressive research team.

His choice of Father Thomas Gaunt, SJ, was brilliant because even before serving as Executive Director of CARA, Father Gaunt had conducted research on the U.S. episcopacy, research that he presented at national sociological conferences. At one of those conferences, Father Fichter told me that he met Sister Catherine Hoegeman, CSJ, a professor at Missouri State University, whose doctoral dissertation on bishops' leadership and decision-making strategies caught his attention. He also reached out to CARA researcher Paul Perl, his co-author from their book on priests and with whom he worked on several *Cultivating Unity* projects around the country.

All throughout the information-gathering process, Father Fichter kept me apprised. He and his team were overjoyed (and I was very pleasantly surprised) when they achieved an impressive 71 percent response rate among us Latin Rite ordinaries and a 67 percent response from the Eastern Rite eparchs. Obviously, my brother bishops trusted CARA's well-deserved reputation as solid non-biased researchers and decided to open up about their lives and their ministries.

Catholic Bishops in the United States is for everyone who is interested in the Catholic Church in our country today. I am sure that the majority of bishops will read it as soon as they get a copy. I can also see many priests and men and women religious doing the same, but what I am most excited about is for the lay faithful to read these pages. My hope is that as they come to know us better they will pray for us all the more fervently at Mass. We certainly need those prayers for, like the famous Bishop of Hippo, we are often "tossed about by stormy activity." Know that as your fellow Christians, we take great comfort in your love, patience, and thoughtful support.

After reading this book, you will know much more about us bishops. So when you next see one of us at a Confirmation, let us know if we are serving you well and if there is anything we can do to improve. And if you ever feel that we need a gentle but firm reminder concerning our sacred duties, encourage us to reread 1 Peter 5:2–3: "Tend the flock of God in your midst, overseeing not by constraint but willingly, as God would have it, not for shameful profit but eagerly. Do not lord it over those assigned to you, but be examples to the flock."

Most Rev. Gregory M. Aymond
14th Archbishop of New Orleans
Chair, CARA Board of Directors

Acknowledgments

THE FOUR OF us would like to thank our families and friends for their support during this multi-year process. We could not have accomplished this goal without them. In addition to them, each of us would like to single out our own sets of especially helpful people.

For Father Stephen, those people are the staff members and parishioners at Sacred Heart (Haworth, NJ) and Saint Elizabeth of Hungary (Wyckoff, NJ) who graciously understood and accepted that he needed quality time away from his pastoral duties to work on this project.

For Father Tom, it is the amazing staff at CARA and his Jesuit community at Georgetown for their support and fellowship. Sister Katie is very grateful for the encouragement of her colleagues at the Department of Sociology and Anthropology at Missouri State University and of her religious community of the Congregation of Saint Joseph. Paul's wife and sons deserve special recognition for sacrificing family time with him on numerous occasions.

Since this is a book about bishops, we want to make special mention (in chronological order) of those bishops who encouraged us: Archbishop Gregory Aymond, Bishop John Flesey, Archbishop John J. Myers, Archbishop Bernard Hebda, and Cardinal Joseph Tobin.

Cardinal Tobin also deserves thanks for agreeing to be one of the four commentators whose insights appear at the end of this book. Along with him, we thank Professor Helen Alvaré, Sister Sharon Euart, RSM, and Father Tom Reese, SJ. You four put the icing on the cake!

We wish that we could list the names of all the bishops who filled out our surveys and who agreed to be interviewed but, since we promised both confidentiality and anonymity, that is not possible. You know who you are. May God reward you for taking time out of your busy schedules to answer our questions! You are the reason this book exists.

Two highly respected researchers, Professor Emeritus Jim Davidson and CARA Senior Researcher Mary Gautier, deserve special credit for their participation in our preliminary meetings when we were trying to figure out which direction we should pursue, and at the end when we needed fresh eyes to make sure that we were not repeating ourselves.

We are also grateful to Felice Goodwin of CARA and Lily Ryan, a CARA student intern, for their painstaking data entry and transcription work, and to Connie Neuman, also at CARA, for her amazing indexing skills.

We thank Cynthia Read, the anonymous reviewers, and the editorial board at Oxford University Press for their guidance. Megan Barnes, Lisa Hroncich, and Judy Kelly did an awesome job as transcribers of our interviews. Kathe Carson, Kathleen Duffy, and Mary Van Dine created an impressive list of book titles and subtitles for which we are deeply grateful. We are also thankful to our proofreaders Lisa Hagy and Nicole Moody.

Finally, we acknowledge the three anonymous families (all from Bergen County, NJ) who generously funded our research efforts. Thank you for believing in the value of our work.

Introduction

CATHOLIC CLERGY ARE a subject of cultural fascination extending beyond the Catholic Church itself. This seems doubly true of bishops, the men who are the priests of the priests, who commission and send them out into the world as Jesus once did. Wearing vestments sometimes reminiscent of kingly raiments, they take a special role in two of Catholicism's holy sacraments. In modern practice (if not strictly in Church law), they alone arise to become the cardinals and popes who are the Church's highest prelates.

Catholic bishops have captured the imagination of novelists, who have fashioned them into unforgettable, larger-than-life characters. These include the saintly Bishop Myriel of *Les Misérables*, the treacherous Cardinal Richelieu of *The Three Musketeers*, the quietly perseverant Bishop Latour of *Death Comes for the Archbishop*, and the scheming Bishop Aringarosa of the popular *The Da Vinci Code*. These portrayals are caricatures, but they reflect a real historical tendency for people, lay Catholics included, to view the bishops on a simplistic spectrum that ranges from haloed hero to biretta'd bad guy. In the European immigrant Church of yesteryear, U.S. Catholics commonly looked up to their bishops with an awe and deference that bordered on reverence. Purdue sociologist Jim Davidson has argued that one of the most important Catholic cultural changes resulting from Vatican II in the 1960s was a willingness for the laity to criticize their leaders. While research conducted by the Center for Applied Research in the Apostolate (CARA) showed that most Catholics approve of the job their own bishop is doing,[1] at the same time Catholics on the left and right alike

---

1. Mark M. Gray and Paul M. Perl, *Catholic Reactions to the News of Sexual Abuse Cases Involving Catholic Clergy* (Washington, DC: Center for Applied Research in the Apostolate, 2006), http://cara.georgetown.edu/Publications/workingpapers/CARAWorkingPaper8.pdf.

now feel little hesitancy in speaking out when they disagree with positions bishops take on issues of the day.

Starting in 2002, the clergy sexual abuse scandal swept away whatever meager dam of deference still inhibited some lay people from criticizing their bishops. The Review Board of lay Catholics appointed to assess the problem in the United States issued a report condemning the bishops' actions in scathing terms.[2] Even before the report was finished, the board's first chairperson resigned after refusing to apologize for his assertion that some of the bishops had acted like "La Cosa Nostra."[3] From outside Catholicism, the assessment was no better: "villains," "criminals," "a medieval dictatorship," and worse appeared in newspapers. One bishop told us how he has seen an intensifying of complaints of all types in recent years: "When I first became bishop people would say, 'I am really worried about Father so-and-so, the way he treats people,' etcetera. But now they say, 'I'm mad about this. You need to move him, and I won't be satisfied until you do.'"

Though the scandal over clergy sexual abuse was a self-inflicted wound, perhaps some of the criticism in other matters has been compounded by the fact that the lives of bishops are not widely known or understood. Our goal in initiating the study behind this book was to ask basic questions about their lives and ministry. What are their favorite aspects of their ministry, their greatest joys and most satisfying relationships? How do they assess and respond to the challenges facing their own dioceses and the U.S. Catholic Church in general? How do they prioritize among the many demands on their time and attention? How do they characterize their relationships with their brother priests or with religious brothers and sisters, and lay people? How will they staff parishes and encourage vocations in

CARA is a Catholic social science research organization founded in 1964 to serve the needs of the U.S. Church. It is located in Washington, DC, and is affiliated with Georgetown University. The chair of its board has always been a bishop or cardinal. However, CARA is not a branch of the USCCB and maintains a great deal of independence in its work. Three of this book's authors are CARA researchers.

2. National Review Board for the Protection of Children and Young People, *A Report on the Crisis in the Catholic Church in the United States* (Washington, DC, 2004), http://www.usccb.org/issues-and-action/child-and-youth-protection/upload/a-report-on-the-crisis-in-the-catholic-church-in-the-united-states-by-the-national-review-board.pdf.

3. Daniel J. Wakin, "Refusing to Recant, Keating Resigns as Church Panel Chief," *New York Times*, June 17, 2003, http://www.nytimes.com/2003/06/17/us/refusing-to-recant-keating-resigns-as-church-panel-chief.html.

the coming years of massive priest retirements? What do they feel about their very public successes and failings? How do they cope with the criticism? We started out with the recognition that they, like us all, are human and that an honest study should acknowledge the complexity of this reality.

Bishops Today

Today's U.S. bishops are an assemblage of paradoxes. Guardians of an ancient religious tradition spanning two millennia, they live fully in a modern world. Excerpts from interviews provide one view of this collage. A bishop listed some of the ways he spreads the word of Jesus: "I give interviews [with the local media], I use the diocesan website, I'm on Facebook. I use those means to reach people." Another described how he prays: "Once in a while I like to pray the Rosary by walking around the lake that's near where I live. I really enjoy that. Or I put on my ear phones and walk around listening to the Divine Office being chanted by some monks in Europe." Still another bishop talked about the amount of time he spends in his car to make parish visits: "When I get back, I always check to see how long my travels are. There have been times when I've put over 1,000 miles on my car in a weekend. This past weekend I put in just under 700 miles. You just have to embrace the drive time or you'll always be on edge." Deeply spiritual men, the bishops often find their time and attention overtaken by waves of managerial challenges and administrative minutia. One said, "Saint Joseph is the saint I turn to most often because we need so much help with our financial problems. . . . I wish that instead of launching a capital campaign to raise money, as we did a few years ago, that we had launched a campaign for spiritual commitment."

Men appointed to positions of power and innumerable responsibilities, many long to spend time with the regular lay Catholics who are ultimately under their care. In reflecting on his change in role from priest to bishop, one bishop said,

> I enjoyed laughing with people. I enjoyed crying with people. I enjoyed visiting people. I enjoyed being a pastor. In that sense it [becoming bishop] was a total break from being a pastor. I wasn't going to be able to do that anymore. . . . I think it still is important to be seen as a pastor. I'm out [at parishes] pretty often; I'm pretty visible. . . . A lot of our people are farmers and ranchers. It's easy to get to the city parishes, but it takes effort and scheduling to get to the

rural parishes, but I do that pretty regularly. I like to be present. I've been here [several] years, and I am proud that I know a lot of people by name. As soon as I get there [to a parish] I catch up quickly on what they're up to.

But, like Jesus, sometimes bishops wish to retreat from the crowd for a time in order to recharge. An archbishop related, "When you're a bishop you are 'on the stage' all the time. For example, I went out last night with a group of priests. They took me out to eat for Christmas and the restaurant was in their parish [boundary]. Looking back on the evening, I think we spent sixty percent of the time talking with their parishioners [who were also at the restaurant]."

The Bishops and Their Role in the Church

Catholicism divides the world into geographic units called dioceses and archdioceses. The men who lead them are bishops and archbishops. The geographic scope and population size should be such that the bishop (with possible assistance) can oversee the ministries and be in relationship with the ministers.[4] Some dioceses, particularly large and populous ones, have auxiliary bishops whose responsibility is to assist the primary bishop (called the "ordinary" in Church parlance).[5] Sometimes auxiliaries are later appointed as ordinaries—typically for another diocese. A very small number of bishops with specialized roles—such as Vatican diplomats—are not attached to a territorial diocese. Dioceses are usually named after the city where the bishop's cathedral church is located—and where the diocesan administrative office ("chancery" or "pastoral center") is also located.

There are currently 177 geographically defined dioceses in the 50 states, District of Columbia, and the U.S. Virgin Islands. The Archdiocese for the Military Services ministers to Catholics in the armed forces, and the Personal Ordinariate of the Chair of St. Peter serves former Anglicans who have entered the Church. The men leading all these entities are the

---

4. Second Vatican Council, *Decree Concerning the Pastoral Office of Bishops in the Church: Christus Dominus*, October 28, 1965, http://www.vatican.va/archive/hist_councils/ii_vatican_council/documents/vat-ii_decree_19651028_christus-dominus_en.html.

5. Strictly speaking, canon law has recently dropped the term *ordinary*. We use it here to avoid potential confusion about the types of bishops we discuss or compare.

"Latin Rite" bishops. At any given time, their number may vary slightly from 179 due to vacancies or the occasional "coadjutor" who works side by side with a bishop and prepares to take over upon his retirement. In recent years, the number of auxiliary bishops serving with the ordinaries has hovered around 70. The bishops (eparchs) of the 18 Eastern Rite Catholic Churches in communion with Rome join with their Latin Rite brothers as members of the United States Conference of Catholic Bishops (USCCB). At the beginning of this project in April 2016, there were 262 active bishops and 168 retired bishops in the United States.

The dioceses in the United States are grouped into 32 provinces. The principle diocese of the province is an archdiocese, and its bishop is an archbishop. Contrary to perceptions we have encountered outside the Church, there is only a limited hierarchy among the U.S. ordinaries. Bishops are under the authority of the pope, but they are individually responsible for their own dioceses.[6] The archbishop provides some leadership for the province, but he does not "oversee" other dioceses or their ordinaries.

Other than size, few important differences exist between territorial dioceses and territorial archdioceses. In most cases in this book, when we say "dioceses" we mean both regular dioceses and archdioceses, and by "the bishops" we mean regular ordinaries and archbishops alike. Cardinals are bishops chosen by the pope to assist him in leading the Church. Their most well-known duty is to vote during a papal conclave. Some are moved by the pope to full-time positions outside of diocesan leadership, but some remain as ordinaries of their dioceses (usually archdioceses). As of 2018, the United States had six cardinal bishops. Again, however, diocesan cardinals have no special role in overseeing their brother bishops.

The U.S. bishops cooperate in many endeavors, but they maintain a great deal of independence and latitude in leading their own dioceses. The bishops meet collectively as a full USCCB assembly twice a year.[7] Together they may decide upon policies to guide themselves (retired bishops do not vote). But, strictly speaking, such policies are not mandatory in the way that canon laws are. Even the most famous set of guidelines adopted by the USCCB in recent years—the *Charter for the Protection of Children*

---

6. Second Vatican Council, *Christus Dominus.*

7. The USCCB offices in Washington, DC are staffed by employees who take care of day-to-day operations. Many bishops travel multiple times throughout the year for USCCB committee obligations.

and Young People[8] of 2002—is enacted voluntarily by the bishops as individuals. So long as they stay within canon law and do not contradict the Church's doctrines, bishops may lead as they see fit.

The Vatican II document on the Pastoral Office of the Bishop, *Christus Dominus*,[9] and the *Catechism of the Catholic Church*[10] describe three primary roles or tasks of the bishop as sanctifying, teaching, and governing. These correspond to the attributes Jesus embodied as priest, prophet, and king.

As sanctifier, a bishop has ultimate responsibility for the provision of the sacraments to Catholics of his diocese. He assumes a special role in two of them: bishops alone confer Holy Orders (the sacrament in which men are ordained to the priesthood); and bishops generally confirm Catholics as full, adult members of the Church. The bishop also presides at a special Mass on Holy Thursday called the Chrism Mass, where he consecrates the holy oil used by his priests. The bishop's mitre (distinctive headwear) is a symbol of priesthood reserved for bishops.

As teacher, a bishop shares with his people the Word of God and instills in them the beliefs of the Catholic Church. This of course includes formal religious education such as Catholic schooling, but also his own preaching, writing, and public statements. The bishop's chair ("cathedra," source of the word *cathedral*) is the primary symbol of his teaching authority.

As governor, a bishop administrates his diocese, which includes managing finances and personnel, and overseeing many other Catholic organizations and initiatives. He is responsible for establishing and staffing parishes, and assigning his diocesan priests to parishes and other ministries. No other members of the clergy, such as religious order priests, may minister within the diocese without his permission. The bishop's staff ("crosier") symbolizes his governing authority. Typically it is fashioned after a shepherd's crook as a reminder of the bishop's pastoral care over the people of his diocese and his duty in gently bringing those who have strayed back into the fold.

There are several other symbols that attach to the bishop. The episcopal ring is a sign of the bishop's figurative marriage to the Church and

---

8. United States Conference of Catholic Bishops, *Charter for the Protection of Children and Young People* (Washington, DC, 2018), http://www.usccb.org/issues-and-action/child-and-youth-protection/upload/Charter-for-the-Protection-of-Children-and-Young-People-2018.pdf.

9. Second Vatican Council, *Christus Dominus*.

10. *Catechism of the Catholic Church* (New York: Doubleday, 1995).

fidelity to his diocese. After a bishop retires or dies, his ring passes to another bishop. The large pectoral cross, which hangs on a chain around his neck, is worn with liturgical vestments and suits to distinguish him from other priests. The coat of arms is another signifier of the bishop's rank in the Church. Coats of arms typically share some common elements, including a shield, a tasseled green hat, a gold cross, and a scroll inscribed with a motto. The symbols on the shield are unique to each bishop. Some bishops take these from their actual family coat of arms; others choose religious symbols that are especially meaningful to them.

Becoming a Bishop

Bishops must be priests first and at least 35 years old. On average, they are priests for about 25 years before they become bishops. The pope chooses priests to become bishops and appoints them to their positions. They typically remain active as bishops until they reach the mandatory retirement age of 75 or until they die. They rarely resign absent serious health problems. Most bishops come from the diocesan priesthood, although a few are members of religious orders. Only a small minority of bishops lead the dioceses where they themselves were ordained as priests. A majority of bishops who serve in their home dioceses are auxiliaries. In many cases, when an ordinary retires or dies, the pope picks a bishop from another diocese to replace him. He typically moves them in a pattern that might be described as upward mobility—from smaller and less populous dioceses to larger ones, where there may be greater administrative challenges and perhaps greater regional or national visibility. This pattern is not without its critics, who argue that bishops should be more familiar with the dioceses they lead, or that bishops may become too concerned with their "careers."

The ordination of a man to the priesthood caps a years-long process of application, internal reflection, external scrutiny, prayer, study of philosophy and theology, pastoral formation, and mentoring from superiors and other priests. Throughout this challenging time he typically receives support from family, friends, parishioners, and perhaps most of all his fellow seminarians. In contrast, the episcopacy thrusts itself upon a priest. The decision to appoint a priest as a new bishop is made quietly by the pope, completely without the knowledge of the man himself. A priest usually learns of the decision no more than a week before his appointment is publicly announced. The process itself is so secretive that many Catholics know little about it other than what is laid out by canon law. The pope chooses a new bishop from among a list of three priests presented to him by the Congregation of Bishops. The only formal requirement is that a priest must be at least 35 years of age and have been ordained for at least five years.

The process of selecting a bishop begins with each ordinary of a province identifying prospective priests. These are usually men from his own diocese, but can be any priests he knows personally. Bishops are encouraged to consult with members of their diocesan priest council and other key clergy or lay people who are knowledgeable about local priests. Consultation must take place privately, one-to-one. Any group consultation is strictly forbidden. Provincial bishops meet to discuss the priests each has identified. These meetings must take place at least every three years but in many provinces typically happen yearly. The names are narrowed to a single list, which is passed up to the apostolic nuncio, the papal ambassador who resides at the Vatican nunciature or embassy in Washington, DC. The nuncio vets candidates by gathering information from people who know them, checking their credentials, reviewing their writings, and so forth. He picks three suitable candidates for each diocese in need of a bishop. The Congregation for Bishops—a Vatican department—reviews the lists and gives the pope three names together with their recommendation for each vacancy. The pope usually accepts this advice, but on occasion he may ask for a recommendation of another name from the list. In the rare instance that a bishop is appointed whose name did not come through normal channels, it is usually a priest who has worked at the Vatican.[11]

Most priests elevated to the episcopacy have some experience in a chancery ministry, such as vicar general or bishop's secretary.[12] Many others have experience in seminary ministry, such as rector or professor. Still, some new bishops have spent most of their priesthood as pastors. Popes seem to exhibit different preferences regarding the background of priests they choose to be bishops. For example, based on our survey data, Pope Benedict XVI and Pope Francis (so far) appointed U.S. bishops with longer

---

11. Ours is a very simplified overview of a rather complex process. This paragraph draws heavily on a much more detailed chapter describing the selection of bishops in Thomas J. Reese, *Archbishop: Inside the Power Structure of the American Catholic Church* (New York: Harper & Row, 1989).

12. A vicar general is the highest officer in a diocese other than a bishop and might be described as a bishop's administrative "right-hand man." A vicar general, as the title implies, must be a priest and is sometimes an auxiliary bishop. Forty percent of ordinaries in our sample have been either a vicar general or bishop's secretary.

average tenures in parish ministry than those appointed by Pope John Paul II.[13]

The reason most commonly given for the secrecy of bishop selection is that it avoids open "campaigns" for episcopal vacancies and the divisiveness that would likely accompany them. Secrecy also relieves potential candidates of the stress an open selection process might bring. Though rarely stated, another benefit is that the most modest and unassuming priests do not remove themselves from candidacy out of humility. But secrecy also brings potential disadvantages. Bishops have little time to prepare for their new ministry.

Bishops who are first appointed as auxiliaries can gain experience working under another bishop. A coadjutor bishop works alongside the ordinary and can learn about his new diocese and its administration before the entire responsibility falls upon his shoulders. Aside from these possibilities, a bishop has to rely mostly on the experiences his priestly ministry has given him. One archbishop said, "I am not sure there is a way to prepare to be a bishop. Even after you are appointed as bishop, there is no quote "bishop school." I think that is one of the weaknesses of the Church—that there really is no immediate mentoring, no immediate workshop or school where you can go and pick things up." The Church has partially addressed this weakness. In 2001, just a few years after this bishop was first appointed, the Congregation for Bishops began an annual seminar with the goal of providing some instruction for how to run their dioceses. All bishops appointed within the prior year are required to attend what some call the "baby bishops' boot camp." Over 150 bishops from around the world participated in the week-long seminar in 2016. Topics included day-to-day issues such as finances, relating to priests, communications and the new media, along with broader issues such as sex abuse prevention and Christians in the Middle East.[14]

---

13. Only 28 percent of current U.S. ordinaries appointed by Pope John Paul II had 15 years in parish ministry (i.e., combined years as a parochial vicar and/or pastor). This compares to 52 percent for Pope Benedict XVI and 57 percent for Pope Francis. Note that most of the active Pope John Paul II bishops in our sample were appointed during the second half of his papacy; those appointed earlier are mostly retired.

14. John Allen, "'Baby Bishops' Get a Crash Course in the Realities of the Church." *Crux*, September 18, 2016, https://cruxnow.com/vatican/2016/09/18/baby-bishops-get-crash-course-realities-church/.

Prior Studies on Priests and Bishops

Social scientists have devoted a great deal of attention to the lives and attitudes of U.S. priests. The first national-level survey of priests was conducted in 1960 by Jesuit sociologist Joseph H. Fichter.[15] Since then, there have been at least nine other academic surveys of priests at the national level.[16] CARA conducted the most recent study in 2009 and reported the findings in the book, *Same Call, Different Men.*[17] A bishop interviewed for this current book lamented that the priesthood is probably the most overly surveyed profession in the country and that he was therefore reluctant to subject his own clergy to more questionnaires. In contrast, no one has yet conducted a social scientific survey of U.S. Catholic bishops. Academic books about them are relatively few and far between. The most important examination of the U.S. bishops is probably the 1989 book *Archbishop,* by Jesuit political scientist and journalist Thomas Reese.[18] Reese synthesized a great deal of existing information about the complex Church laws, procedures, and traditions that guide the ministry of the bishops. He built upon this by interviewing the 31 archbishops and hundreds of other individuals in the Church hierarchy and administration. Our hope at the outset of this project was to provide an expanded and updated view by surveying all of the bishops and asking a wider range of questions about them. Some questions in the survey are similar in scope to those of the recent priest surveys and allow for comparisons between priests and bishops; others focus on aspects specific to the episcopacy.

Data Used in This Study

The central source of data for this book is a survey conducted in 2016. It appears in Appendix A. Before it was finalized, three bishops who are friends to CARA reviewed it and provided suggestions. In April 2016, we mailed the questionnaire to all active and retired, Latin and Eastern Rite

---

15. Joseph H. Fichter, *America's Forgotten Priests: What They Are Saying* (New York: Harper & Row, 1968). Joseph Fichter is the granduncle of this book's first author, Stephen Fichter.

16. Additionally, *The Los Angeles Times* conducted two of its own surveys which became the basis of a book by priest sociologist Andrew M. Greeley, *Priests: A Calling Crisis* (Chicago: University of Chicago Press, 2004).

17. Mary L. Gautier, Paul M. Perl, and Stephen J. Fichter, *Same Call, Different Men: The Evolution of the Priesthood since Vatican II* (Collegeville, MN: Liturgical Press, 2012).

18. Reese, *Archbishop.*

U.S. bishops. In compiling a mailing list for the bishops we used the 2016 *Official Catholic Directory* (*OCD*).[19] A cover letter explained the purpose of the project and guaranteed confidentiality of responses. The letter was printed on CARA letterhead and signed by Gaunt as CARA's executive director. It was decided by USSCB leadership that an official posture of neutrality would best serve the interests of the Conference, so the survey did not receive a formal USCCB endorsement. However, we are very grateful to a few prominent bishops who privately encouraged participation among their brothers.

To preserve the anonymity of responses, we included a postcard the bishops could mail back separately to let us know they had completed and returned their questionnaires. In May, 2016 we sent a follow-up mailing with a second copy of the questionnaire to those who had not yet returned the postcards. We completed data collection in October and obtained the response rates shown in Table I.1.

We are pleased with the response rates for ordinaries, which are similar to the rates obtained by the best national-level mailed surveys of priests. For example, Hoge and Wenger's 2001 survey of priests in selected dioceses and religious orders obtained a response rate of 71 percent.[20] The low response rate for retired bishops may be partly due to inaccuracies with addresses or from health issues among some of these men. The lower response of auxiliaries relative to ordinaries is more difficult to explain but may reflect the fact that some questions in the survey focus on the role of the ordinary and do not apply as well to the ministry of auxiliaries.

Table I.1 Survey Response Rates by Bishop Type

	Surveys Sent	Responses	Response Rate (%)
Latin Rite ordinaries	179	127	71
Eastern Rite ordinaries	18	12	67
Auxiliary bishops	65	33	51
Retired bishops	168	42	25

---

19. *The Official Catholic Directory*, Vol. 2016 (New Providence, NJ: P.J. Kenedy & Sons, 2016). Sometimes called the Kenedy Directory, after its publisher.

20. Dean R. Hoge and Jacqueline E. Wenger, *Evolving Visions of the Priesthood: Changes from Vatican II to the Turn of the New Century* (Collegeville, MN: Liturgical Press, 2003). See page 3.

For the Latin Rite ordinaries,[21] we compared the survey respondents to the nonrespondents on various characteristics. See Appendix B for details. The only significant difference is related to the size of the diocese. Respondents were more likely to be from smaller dioceses than from larger ones.

This book reports findings predominantly for Latin Rite ordinaries.[22] A fair and thorough discussion of all the different types of bishops lies beyond the scope of a single volume. We chose instead to focus on the bishops who currently hold decision-making power in the Church. Appendix C provides comparisons of responses between the different types of bishops for some key survey questions.

We supplemented the survey with telephone or face-to-face interviews of 13 bishops—ten active Latin Rite ordinaries, one Eastern Rite ordinary, one auxiliary bishop, and one retired bishop. Some of these bishops were individuals known to one or more of us through work or ministry. To move beyond our personal networks, we drew a small random sample of ordinaries and sent each a letter asking if he would be willing to speak with us. About half the interviewees were recruited this way. We conducted the phone interviews from December 2016 to April 2017. We recorded the interviews with the permission of respondents and transcribed them verbatim. We present selected quotes from these interviews (with modest editing for grammar, clarity, and brevity) throughout the book.

We also draw on some additional data sources. Some general information about the bishops and their dioceses comes from the OCD[23] (the 2016 edition unless noted otherwise). Gaunt used diocesan websites and Wikipedia to compile a database of demographic and educational information for active Latin Rite bishops as of April 2016.[24] References to trends over time come from longitudinal data on bishops and dioceses compiled by Hoegeman from the 1983–2016 *OCD*[25], internet searches on bishops,

---

21. Data necessary to do this for the other groups had not been compiled.

22. A few exceptions are noted in the text.

23. *The Official Catholic Directory*.

24. Thomas P. Gaunt, Database of Bishop Demographic and Educational Information from Diocesan Websites (Washington, DC: Center for Applied Research in the Apostolate, 2016).

25. Catherine Hoegeman, Bishop Information Database, 1978–2017. (Springfield, MO: Missouri State University, 2017).

and the Catholic-Hierarchy.org website.[26] We collected information about diocesan policies and planning from diocesan websites in June/July 2017.

Organization of the Book

This book includes seven primary chapters followed by four commentaries. The first chapter provides facts about current U.S. bishops, including demographics and the characteristics of the dioceses they lead. Some of the facts we present are existing information taken from the *OCD*. And we are also pleased to present some new, previously unavailable information from the survey.

Insofar as a person as busy as a Catholic bishop can ever have a "typical" day, what does it look like? Chapter 2 explores a day in the life of a bishop. What tasks occupy his time? How much time does he spend in prayer? How does he juggle so many meetings and special events? From what sources does he get his secular and ecclesiastical news? These and many other questions are covered in this chapter.

Chapter 3 seeks to understand the greatest sources of satisfaction for bishops. Where do they find joy and happiness in their ministry and in their private lives? Some of the survey items we use to answer this question have been previously asked of priests. This allows us to investigate ways in which bishops and priests are similar to and different from each other.

In Chapter 4 we share the bishops' reflections in response to two of the open-ended questions in the survey. The first question asked about the greatest challenges facing the U.S. Church today. Complementing the first, a second question asked bishops to identify the greatest sources of hope they see for the future of the Church. Vocations to the priesthood were mentioned related to both hopes and challenges, so this chapter also explores how bishops are encouraging vocations in an age when far fewer people are going into the priesthood and religious life.

Chapter 5 discusses personnel issues and collaboration. How do bishops describe their working relationships with the clergy, religious sisters and brothers, and laity in their dioceses? How do they balance being both a pastor and a "boss" to their diocesan priests? What groups of priests and laity do bishops consult with when making important decisions?

---

26. David M. Cheney, Catholic-Hierarchy (2017). http://www.catholic-hierarchy.org/country/us.html.

Chapter 6 examines the episcopal role of governance and administration. It focuses on the ways bishops are staffing parishes in a time of fewer priests and how they are addressing long-term administrative challenges through pastoral planning processes.

As teachers of the faith and the public face of Catholicism, bishops speak out on many issues of the day. Chapter 7 examines the topics bishops address when they write to Catholics of their dioceses and the extent to which they take a public stance with regard to political advocacy or voting. We also asked bishops in interviews how they deal with the criticism that often comes with taking a stand on controversial issues.

Note that while there is not a separate chapter dedicated to the sexual abuse scandal, sections of Chapters 4, 6, and 7 discuss it. Our intention is not to minimize this important topic, but the space necessary to fully analyze and reflect upon it would require a separate book.

The final section of the book presents commentaries from four individuals of varied backgrounds who are knowledgeable and respected leaders in the Church: Professor Helen Alvaré; Sister Sharon Euart, RSM; Father Thomas Reese, SJ; and Cardinal Joseph Tobin, CSsR. They share reactions and provide greater insight on the findings we have presented.

Who Are the Bishops and Where Do They Come From?

Therefore, a bishop must be irreproachable, married only once, temperate, self-controlled, decent, hospitable, able to teach, not a drunkard, not aggressive, but gentle, not contentious, not a lover of money. He must manage his own household well, keeping his children under control with perfect dignity; for if a man does not know how to manage his own household, how can he take care of the church of God? He should not be a recent convert, so that he may not become conceited and thus incur the devil's punishment. He must also have a good reputation among outsiders, so that he may not fall into disgrace, the devil's trap.

I TIMOTHY 3:2–7

In regard to the suitability of a candidate for the episcopacy, it is required that he is: outstanding in solid faith, good morals, piety, zeal for souls, wisdom, prudence, and human virtues, and endowed with other qualities which make him suitable to fulfill the office in question; of good reputation; at least thirty-five years old; ordained to the presbyterate for at least five years; in possession of a doctorate or at least a licentiate in sacred scripture, theology, or canon law from an institute of higher studies approved by the Apostolic See, or at least truly expert in the same disciplines.

CODE OF CANON LAW, Canon 378 §1.

ONE OF THE earliest descriptions of the characteristics of a bishop is found in St. Paul's First Letter to Timothy. St. Paul emphasizes that a bishop be irreproachable and have a good reputation. The bishop should be a good manager and not a recent convert. A more recent description of a bishop is found in the Code of Canon Law, and it repeats many of the same attributes, stressing that the bishop be outstanding in Christian virtues and well suited for the office. Canon law additionally requires a minimum age for a bishop, that he be a priest for at least five years, and have a high level of formal education.

These are the aspirations for a bishop from the earliest days of the Church to the current time. How well do they fit the reality of human limitations? In trying to assess and identify the desired qualities for a bishop, some criteria are hard to measure and instead rely on a careful, discerning judgment (solid faith, gentleness, wisdom, etc.); other criteria are more readily ascertained and documented (age, management skills, education, etc.).

This chapter provides an overview of information on the bishops and examines the readily documented details of the current bishops of the United States: their age, where they are from, where they went to school, and what they studied. Additionally, what is the size and complexity of the dioceses they lead? Characteristics such as these are helpful in understanding the human, cultural, and geographic context of the American bishops at the start of the 21st century.[1]

How Many Bishops Are There?

In April 2016 there were 430 bishops, in active ministry or retired, in 197 archdioceses, dioceses, and eparchies in the 50 states, the District of Columbia, and the U.S. Virgin Islands. Latin Rite dioceses make up 178 of the dioceses, 18 are Eastern Rite, and there is one Personal Ordinariate of the Chair of St. Peter for the former Anglicans who have entered the Church.[2]

There were 65 Latin Rite auxiliary bishops serving in 30 of the 178 dioceses. Twenty-nine of these 30 dioceses with auxiliary bishops are among

---

1. All of the data on the number of dioceses, bishops, priests, and parishes are taken from *The Official Catholic Directory*, Vol. 2016 (New Providence, NJ: P.J. Kenedy & Sons, 2016).

2. Thomas P. Gaunt, Bishop Demographic and Educational Information from Diocesan Websites [Data file]. Washington, DC: Center for Applied Research in the Apostolate, 2016.

the 50 largest dioceses in the country. Large dioceses without an auxiliary bishop include the dioceses of San Bernardino, Orange, Fresno, and San Diego in California, and Brownsville in Texas, each with more than 1,000,000 Catholics.

Almost four in ten living bishops are retired (168, or 39 percent). Among the remaining active bishops, 178 are Latin Rite ordinaries (the head of their diocese), assisted by 65 auxiliary bishops. The Eastern Rite eparchies have 18 ordinaries and one auxiliary bishop.

As of 2016, 45 percent of the current Latin Rite ordinaries were appointed as bishop by Pope John Paul II, 42 percent by Pope Benedict XVI, and the remaining 13 percent by Pope Francis. On average, about three or four percent of the ordinaries are replaced each year. Including Pope Benedict XVI's eight-year tenure between Pope John Paul II and Pope Francis, the most common pattern is that when a bishop named by the previous pope steps down, his replacement is named by the next pope.

What Are the Dioceses They Lead?

The 178 Latin Rite dioceses of the United States are grouped into 32 ecclesial provinces, or geographical areas, usually including one or more states and having two or more dioceses. California and Texas each contain multiple provinces. An archdiocese is the main diocese of the ecclesial province and often the more prominent city of that region. Each province is named after its territorial archdiocese.[3] The Archdiocese for the Military Services is an additional non-territorial archdiocese, bringing the total number of U.S. provinces to 33. In 2015, the Latin Rite dioceses counted 63,055,943 parish-identified Catholics ranging from the Diocese of Juneau with 10,000 Catholics to the Archdiocese of Los Angeles with 4,029,336. About half of the dioceses had fewer than 200,000 Catholics, and 19 dioceses had more than 1,000,000. In the least populous dioceses it is not unusual for the bishop to be at any given parish once or twice a year. In the most populous dioceses, however, the bishop is fortunate if he is able to visit a parish more than once every three or more years. Figure 1.1 shows

---

3. An Ecclesiastical Province is a defined geographic area containing an archdiocese, or Metropolitan See, and at least one diocese, or Suffragen See. The archbishop of the archdiocese has no direct powers over the Suffragen Sees, but does have limited advisory and appellate authority and obligations.

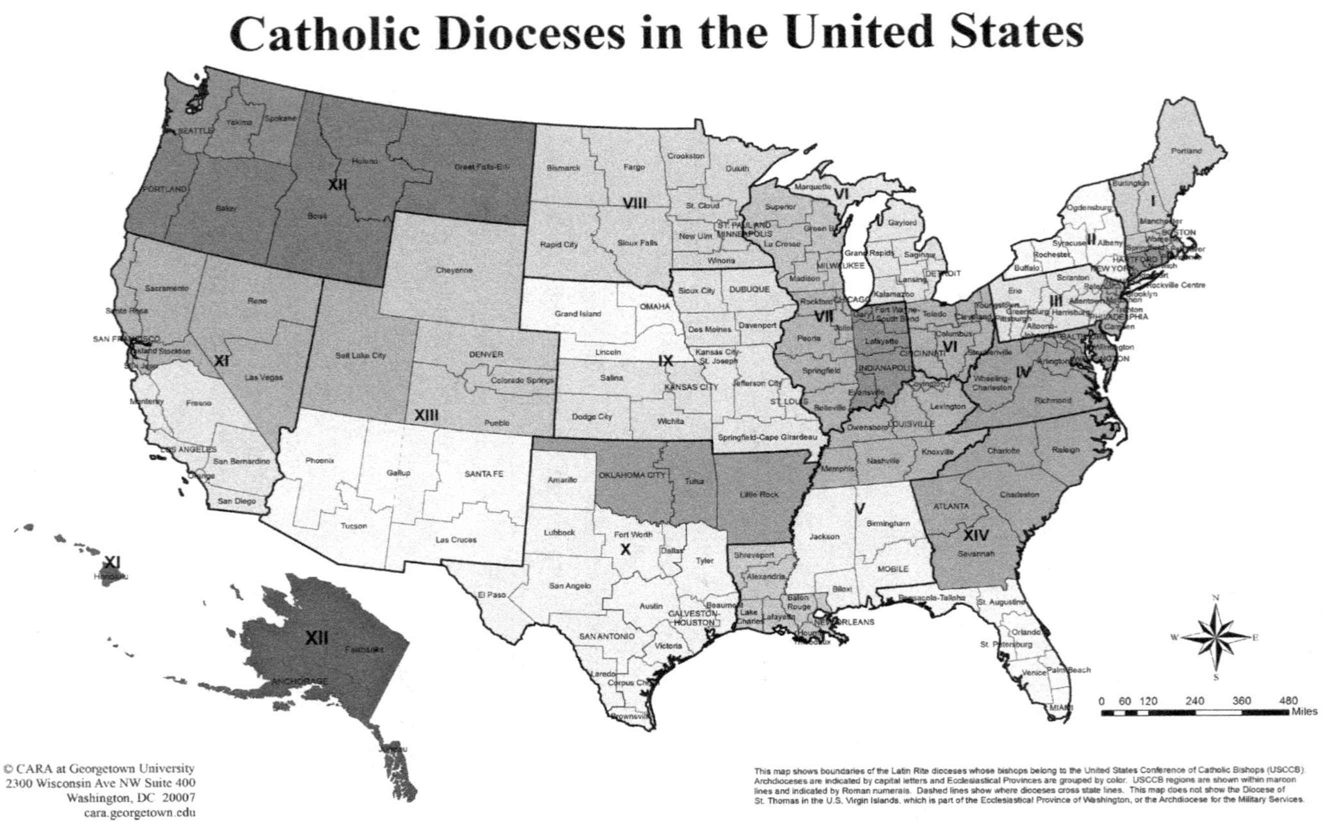

Catholic Dioceses in the United States

This map shows boundaries of the Latin Rite dioceses whose bishops belong to the United States Conference of Catholic Bishops (USCCB). Archdioceses are indicated by capital letters and Ecclesiastical Provinces are grouped by color. USCCB regions are shown within maroon lines and indicated by Roman numerals. Dashed lines show where dioceses cross state lines. This map does not show the Diocese of St. Thomas in the U.S. Virgin Islands, which is part of the Ecclesiastical Province of Washington, or the Archdiocese for the Military Services.

FIGURE 1.1 Map of United States Dioceses

Source: CARA 2017.

a map of the United States Latin Rite dioceses, highlighting geographical size differences.

The 18 Eastern Rite eparchies each cover multiple states, or even the entire nation, and count a total of 630,000 Catholics. The smallest is the Byzantine Catholic Eparchy of Phoenix, with 2,400 Catholics in 13 western states, and the largest is the Chaldean Eparchy of Saint Thomas the Apostle, with 180,000 Catholics in the eastern half of the United States.

The United States includes 16,255 parishes and the median (midpoint) number of parishes per diocese is 81. The Diocese of St. Thomas, Virgin Islands is the smallest diocese, with only eight parishes, and the Archdiocese of Chicago is the largest, with 351 parishes. The average number of Catholics per parish nationwide is 4,027, but this varies greatly. The Diocese of Fairbanks averages 271 Catholics per parish compared to the Diocese of Orange in California, which averages 23,624 Catholics per parish. Thirty-one dioceses have less than 1,000 Catholics per parish, while 16 dioceses have more than 10,000 Catholics per parish.

Table 1.1 lists the ten largest and ten smallest dioceses of the United States. The ten largest combined have more than 70 times as many Catholics as the ten smallest dioceses. The scale and complexity of dioceses are vastly different across the country.[4] The annual operating budgets of

Table 1.1 2015 Catholic Population of Ten Largest and Smallest Dioceses

10 Largest Dioceses	Number of Catholics	10 Smallest Dioceses	Number of Catholics
Los Angeles, CA	4,029,336	Baker, OR	36,994
New York, NY	2,642,740	Alexandria, LA	36,280
Chicago, IL	2,228,000	Great Falls-Billings, MT	33,703
Boston, MA	1,954,201	Steubenville, OH	33,469
Galveston-Houston, TX	1,723,062	Crookston, MN	32,089
San Bernardino, CA	1,671,967	St. Thomas, VI	30,000
Brooklyn, NY	1,506,000	Anchorage, AK	27,345
Rockville Centre, NY	1,455,644	Rapid City, SD	26,462
Philadelphia, PA	1,438,147	Fairbanks, AK	12,475
Orange, CA	1,346,540	Juneau, AK	10,000

Source: Official Catholic Directory, 2016.

4. *The Official Catholic Directory.*

dioceses vary greatly as well, with the smallest dioceses reporting budgets of less than $2,000,000 and the largest dioceses reporting budgets of more than $80,000,000—and this excludes the budgets of their Catholic Charities![5]

The number of diocesan priests and deacons serving in a diocese varies from ten priests in the Diocese of Juneau to 772 priests in the Archdiocese of Chicago. The Diocese of Lincoln has only two deacons, while the Archdiocese of Chicago has 652 deacons.

Catholics make up at least 21 percent of the population in the United States, but some regions of the country are far less Catholic than others. Catholics are less than 3 percent of the population in the dioceses of Jackson, Savannah, Knoxville, and Lexington, but more than 70 percent of the population in the dioceses of Corpus Christi, El Paso, Brownsville, and Laredo—all in Texas. The cultural and ethnic diversity of the Catholic population can also vary widely from diocese to diocese. This diversity generally corresponds to the immigration patterns across the nation, which are closely linked to economic opportunities—as is seen in many dioceses across the South and West. A bishop from an eastern diocese reflects on the size and diversity of his diocese:

> Parishioners don't realize how big the archdiocese is. We have more than 1,100 buildings in the archdiocese. When I do Confirmations and go from an all Korean parish, to an all black one, to an all Spanish one, and to an all white one, you realize that the number of cultures interacting within this archdiocese is amazing. It is a tremendous responsibility to be the archbishop in such a large archdiocese.

In addition to overall growth in size, the Catholic population has also been quite mobile in recent decades, moving from the large urban centers to the suburbs, and from the Northeast and Midwest to the South and West.[6] While many of the dioceses of the Northeast and Midwest experience a stable or diminishing Catholic population, dioceses in the South

---

5. Michal J. Kramarek and Thomas P. Gaunt, *National Diocesan Survey: Salary and Benefits for Priests and Lay Personnel 2017* (Washington, DC: National Association of Church Personnel Administrators, 2017), 14.

6. Charles E. Zech, Mary L. Gautier, Mark M. Gray, Jonathon L. Wiggins, and Thomas P. Gaunt, *Catholic Parishes of the 21st Century* (New York: Oxford University Press, 2017), 9.

and West more typically experience rapid growth in Catholic population. Table 1.2 provides a few examples showing that dioceses in the Northeast have declined by more than 125,000 Catholics over 20 years, while dioceses in the South and West have grown by more than 800,000 Catholics in the same period. A diocese with declining numbers or one with explosive growth present very different pastoral challenges for the local bishop.

Table 1.2 Sample of Dioceses Population Growth and Decline

Diocese	Number of Catholics in 1995	Number of Catholics in 2015	Change	% Change
Buffalo	755,427	601,563	− 153,864	− 20%
Pittsburgh	760,697	632,138	− 128,559	− 17%
Cleveland	825,356	682,948	− 142,408	− 17%
San Bernardino	610,736	1,671,967	+ 1,061,231	+ 174%
Dallas	319,631	1,320,737	+ 1,001,106	+ 313%
Atlanta	212,850	1,023,594	+ 810,744	+ 381%

Source: Official Catholic Directory, 1996, 2016.

How Old Are They?

As of 2016, the Latin Rite ordinaries, on average, are 65 years old. One-quarter are 70 or older, one-half of the bishops are in their 60s, one-quarter are under 60 years of age, and just two are under 50. On average, they have been a bishop for 12 years and were ordained to the priesthood when they were 27 years old. It is unusual for a priest to be named a bishop if he is under age 40 or over 65; only 2 percent of the bishops were that young or old when appointed.[7]

The 65 auxiliary bishops have an average age of 61, have been a bishop for five years, and were ordained to the priesthood at age 30. Overall, the auxiliary bishops tend to be ordained as a priest and as bishops three years later than the average ordinary.

Usually six to eight ordinaries reach the retirement age of 75 each year. The retired bishops are 82 years old, on average, and were younger than

---

7. Gaunt, Database of Bishop Information.

current active ordinaries when ordained to the priesthood (age 25) but became bishops at the same age (age 53).

Where Are They From?

Nearly all Latin Rite ordinaries were born in the United States, only seven were born elsewhere (five in Latin America and two in Ireland).[8] A little more than one in ten are Hispanic, African American, Asian, or Native American.

By and large, most bishops are not native to the state where they are serving. Two-thirds of the bishops came to a diocese from outside that state or geographic region. Just over one-third of the bishops serve either in the dioceses in which they were ordained as a priest or in a neighboring diocese of the same ecclesial province. Only 11 bishops serve in the same diocese in which they were ordained as a priest, and another 54 serve as ordinaries within the same ecclesial province where they were priests.

A bishop from a diocese in the South commented:

Unfortunately, coming from another part of the country you do not know anybody. The advantage is there is no baggage, there is not a history with anyone, so it's really *tabula rasa* in that regard and so you have a chance to build with no issues [compared to one] being in the diocese for your entire priesthood. Of course, the disadvantage on the other end is that in not knowing anyone there is a little uncertainty because you just do not know. That was a big adjustment, as much as coming to a diocese that I have never even visited that state before, let alone the diocese. And in that sense adjusting to a whole different history of a mission diocese compared to [my home] which is a more traditional diocese.

Some ecclesial provinces produce many more bishops than the proportionate size of their Catholic population. The Province of Philadelphia (encompassing the eight dioceses of Pennsylvania) produced 22 of the current bishops, and the Province of Chicago (encompassing the six dioceses of Illinois) produced 11 bishops. In contrast, the Province of Santa Fe, encompassing five dioceses of New Mexico and Arizona, has produced

8. Ibid.

no current ordinary. The Provinces of Anchorage, Atlanta, Indianapolis, Mobile, and Portland have each produced one current ordinary.

In 2016, fewer than 10 percent of the active ordinaries come from religious orders. Among the 16 religious order bishops are three Conventual Franciscans, three members of the Society of Divine Word, two Capuchin Franciscans, two Jesuits, and one bishop each from the Oblates of Mary Immaculate, Congregation of the Mission, Redemptorists, Missionaries of the Holy Spirit, Congregation of the Holy Cross, and Claretians.

Where Did They Go to School and What Did They Study?

Just under one-quarter of the bishops attended a public high school, one-half went to a Catholic high school, and about one-quarter attended a high school minor seminary.[9] The proportion of older bishops named by Pope John Paul II who attended a public high school is much smaller— only 9 percent—compared to the one-third or more of younger bishops named by Pope Benedict XVI and Pope Francis. In contrast, two-fifths of the bishops appointed by Pope John Paul II attended a high school minor seminary, while only about one in ten bishops appointed by Pope Benedict XVI and Pope Francis did. During the past decade or so, the high school experience of newly appointed bishops is beginning to resemble more and more the experience of Catholic laity.[10]

Practically all of the bishops received their undergraduate education at a Catholic institution of higher learning. A little more than one-half of the bishops attended a seminary for their undergraduate college education, nearly one-third attended a Catholic college or university, and only one in eight attended a public institution. Just a handful of bishops attended a private non-Catholic institution. About half of the bishops studied in Rome at some point, either for initial seminary work or for graduate degrees.

Table 1.3 compares undergraduate majors based on the types of colleges the bishops attended. Their fields of study are diverse, especially among those 43 percent who did not attend undergraduate seminaries. One-half of the bishops earned an undergraduate degree in philosophy, primarily those who attended a college seminary. One-quarter earned degrees in the

---

9. Ibid.

10. The CARA Catholic Poll in 2012 reported that 21 percent of Catholics had attended a Catholic high school.

Table 1.3 Undergraduate Majors by Type of College Attended

Major	Seminary (%)	Catholic (%)	Public (%)	Private (%)	Total (%)
Philosophy	72	47	5	0	52
Humanities	21	20	42	100	26
STEM	0	13	32	0	9
Business	2	10	21	0	7
Theology	5	10	0	0	6

Source: Gaunt Bishop Information Database, 2016.

humanities, social sciences, or arts. Fewer than one in ten earned a degree in the STEM fields (Science, Technology, Engineering, Mathematics), in business, accounting, or finance, or in theology or religious studies.

As a whole, the bishops are a highly educated group of leaders within the United States. The 175 bishops hold more than 368 graduate degrees, with 124 of them (71 percent) having three or more graduate degrees. Among these degrees, 294 are at the Masters or Licentiate level (a comparable academic degree conferred by a Pontifical University), and most of these are in theology or canon law.

Two-thirds of the 74 earned doctoral level degrees are ecclesial degrees in theology, canon law, or liturgy. Seven bishops have civil law degrees, and one has a doctorate in education. Eighteen of the bishops have PhDs in the areas of history, human development, biblical theology, ethics, and political science.

The interviews included questions asking about any college or graduate courses that bishops felt were particularly helpful in preparing them for their ministry as bishop, or courses they wished they had taken. The bishops had a variety of responses. One bishop focused on specific academic courses:

> Well in graduate studies, certainly my scripture classes. I studied at the Gregorian University in Rome and really treasured my scripture classes. I still tap into that experience preparing for homilies.

In contrast, another bishop focused on the more pastoral aspects:

> For me, but this is my bent, would be mostly the pastoral courses. You need theological knowledge and you need theological acumen

to be able to teach and preach. But in my mind, it's not just about knowing theology. It's how you teach and preach and how you work with people. And, I think the pastoral courses gave me the grounding for that.

A Midwestern bishop reflected that the formation aspects of seminary were probably more valuable than the academics. He went on to describe some specific aspects of formation:

Spiritual direction, deepening one's spiritual life, that was always very helpful. Participating regularly in Mass and the spiritual exercises. And then on the other hand, having someone who tends to be challenged in one's behavior is always good. Plus, I would lay a third element, the community itself. Being with one's peers, seminarians or fellow seminarians, is very formative as well. Those are the things that have had more of an impact on me as a priest and as a bishop, than I suppose as the academics part. I studied Philosophy that lays the groundwork as you know for Theology; so maybe, I am underplaying the academics too much here.

A bishop from the Midwest recognized the benefit of philosophy and theology as well as more practically oriented courses:

The few years I had of Spanish came back to laying some remote foundation from many years ago, because I now have a facility with Spanish. I'm not fluent, but it is adequate. I think practically speaking that was a good thing. I think in general the philosophy and theology course of study, you know what they say about philosophy, you learn to be a little more critical and reflective and I think that's important as a bishop, as a pastor. You know even more so as a bishop you continually have to step back and reflect on personnel, on the direction of the diocese, or specific events within the diocese, aging priests, resources, and finances.

A recently appointed ordinary noted that his qualification to be bishop was not dependent on advanced degrees:

I have no special degrees, I never studied in Rome or anything like that. I'm a local yokel. . . . I say I have no qualifications to be a bishop. I don't have any advanced degrees, canon law degrees, I'm a product of our farm system and now I'm in the big leagues.

One bishop from a diocese in the West commented that he found his work experience far more valuable than his college courses.

I started working when I was thirteen years old and have to say my work experience was helpful. I worked at a drycleaners, I balanced the till every night. I spent seven years working at an insurance company and I paid my way through college. And working in insurance, I learned about health insurance and claims. . . . So I really learned about budgets, spreadsheets, and some of it on the administrative side, I didn't get any of that in college or in seminary. I got all of that from working. . . . I look to my work experience for how to bring together the Gospel with the material day to day.

What Did They Do Before Becoming a Bishop?

The ministerial background of bishops varies from parish work, to diocesan administration, to seminary education. Table 1.4 shows bishops' prior roles, compared across the different popes who appointed them.

Almost all of the bishops we surveyed have five or more years of experience in parish ministry as either a pastor or parochial vicar (associate pastor).

Table 1.4 Positions Prior to Being a Bishop by the Pope that Appointed Them

"Prior to Episcopacy, were you a . . .?"	John Paul II (%)	Benedict XVI (%)	Francis (%)	Overall (%)
Parochial Vicar	90	98	91	93
Pastor	62	90	91	76
Professor	34	25	36	31
Seminary Rector	23	18	18	21
Bishop's Secretary	21	12	0	16
Chancellor	18	22	0	18
Vicar General	30	37	46	34

Note: Totals do not add up to 100% because bishops typically held multiple prior positions.

Source: CARA Bishop Survey, 2016.

Ninety-three percent have been a parochial vicar, and 76 percent have been a pastor. Bishops named by Pope Benedict and Pope Francis are more likely than those named by Pope John Paul II to have served as the pastor of a parish.

A retired bishop commented briefly on what is perhaps an obvious benefit of having the shared experience with his priests:

> I think that [being vicar of priests] was very advantageous. I also think being a pastor myself helped me because the majority of priests that a bishop has to oversee are pastors. I understood their plights and the difficulties of running a parish and the difficulties dealing with the public, and so on and so forth.

Three in ten bishops were previously professors (most often in seminaries), and one in five were the rector of a seminary. Interestingly, Pope Benedict XVI, who spent many years as a theology professor, was less likely than Pope John Paul II, and no more likely than Pope Francis, to name a bishop who had been a professor or the rector of a seminary. A bishop from a diocese in the South reflected on his prior seminary experience:

> Certainly, my work in high school helped me develop a style of teaching and a comfortability with young people. That's helped me in many ways. In my work at the seminary I had a lot of time to reflect on the priesthood, the meaning of the priesthood, dealing with and working with seminarians and young priests. And, quite frankly it also developed my own spirituality and identity as a priest. So, the work in a seminary not only was in many ways administrative, especially when I served as rector, but also it gave me spiritual opportunities and the opportunity to work with a lot of bishops as we had over 20 dioceses that were sending us seminarians.

Overall, 62 percent of current ordinaries served in some form of diocesan administration prior to becoming a bishop. Common positions include vicar general, chancellor, judicial vicar, vicar for clergy, or bishop's secretary.[11] About one-third of the bishops have served as the vicar general,

---

11. The bishop is required to appoint a vicar general for the diocese. As described earlier, a vicar general is the second highest official in a diocese after the bishop, and must be a priest. He handles many of the administrative tasks of the bishop. A chancellor is a diocesan record keeper and archivist. A diocesan administrator temporarily oversees a diocese when a bishop has retired or died but a new bishop has not yet been appointed. A judicial vicar is a canon lawyer who handles diocesan issues of Church law and oversees its tribunal (ecclesiastical

and not quite one in five served as the chancellor of a diocese, bishop's secretary, or other administrative roles. One in five bishops named by Pope John Paul II was a secretary to a bishop, about one in ten for Pope Benedict XVI, and none so far for Pope Francis.

Among the bishops who are currently ordinaries, 42 percent went from being a priest directly to ordinary of a diocese, 6 percent initially served as a coadjutor bishop,[12] 42 percent served as an auxiliary bishop first, and two current ordinaries were serving as a Vatican official when they were first appointed bishop. For almost 29 percent of the bishops, their current position is their second or subsequent assignment as an ordinary.

How Do They Describe Their Theological Perspective?

Within the unity of Catholic doctrine and teaching, there is a range of theological perspectives. Although it is difficult to formally define what distinguishes traditional, moderate, and progressive perspectives, there is a general understanding that these differences exist. The survey asked bishops, "How would others describe your general theological orientation?" Among the current bishops, 42 percent think others perceive them as traditional. Practically equal to this, 41 percent think others perceive them moderate. The remaining 17 percent identified as progressive.

Table 1.5 displays the responses for active Latin Rite ordinaries compared across the different popes who appointed them. It may seem that, compared to his predecessors, Pope Francis appointed more traditional and moderate bishops and fewer progressive ones. However, there is not a statistically significant difference in bishops' theological orientations based on which pope appointed them. The comparison is difficult due to the notable differences in the relative number of bishops appointed by each pope. Of the 127 survey respondents, Pope John Paul II appointed 51 percent, Pope Benedict XVI appointed 39 percent, and Pope Francis appointed 10 percent. Pope Francis' emphasis in selecting bishops is based on their having a pastoral orientation, which is not dependent on a particular theological orientation.

---

court). A vicar for clergy provides assistance to the priests and deacons of the diocese and helps the bishop with priest assignments and priest personnel issues.

12. A coadjutor is a bishop assigned to assist a current ordinary and who has right of succession when the current ordinary retires.

Table 1.5 **Bishops' Theological Orientation by Pope that Appointed Them**

Theological Orientation	John Paul II (%)	Benedict XVI (%)	Francis (%)	Overall (%)
Traditional	39	42	58	42
Moderate	39	48	25	41
Progressive	23	10	17	17

Source: CARA Bishop Survey, 2016.

Which pope appointed a bishop is influenced by time period and, therefore, by birth and ordination cohorts. Following prior priest surveys,[13] we used four cohorts to distinguish the bishops based on the year of their ordination to the priesthood. Pre-Vatican II includes those ordained prior to 1964. The Vatican II cohort is between 1964 and 1977. Post-Vatican II covers the first half of the pontificate of Pope John Paul II, 1978–1991. Priests ordained after 1991 are the millennial cohort. Priests from the Vatican II cohort are more likely to be progressive, while priests from the pre-Vatican II, post-Vatican II, and millennial cohorts tend to be more traditional.[14] Each pope had different cohorts of priests to choose from. Pope Francis is less likely to have appointed bishops who are from the Vatican II priest ordination cohort and more likely to have appointed bishops from the post-Vatican II and millennial cohorts. None of the 127 survey respondents are from the pre-Vatican II cohort and eight are among the millennial cohort. Therefore, we collapsed the four ordination cohort categories into two, combining pre-Vatican II with Vatican II, and post-Vatican II with millennial. Table 1.6 displays the responses for active Latin Rite ordinaries compared between these two groups. There is not a statistically significant difference in theological orientation based on priesthood ordination cohort. While prior research shows theological differences among priests based on ordination cohort, this might be less true for bishops.

13. Mary L. Gautier, Paul M. Perl, and Stephen J. Fichter, *Same Call, Different Men: The Evolution of the Priesthood since Vatican II* (Collegeville, MN: Liturgical Press, 2012).

14. Dean R. Hoge and Jacqueline E. Wenger, *Evolving Visions of the Priesthood: Changes from Vatican II to the Turn of the New Century* (Collegeville, MN: Liturgical Press, 2003).

Table 1.6 Theological Orientation by Priest Ordination Cohort

	Pre /Vatican II (%)	Post-Vatican II / Millennial (%)	Overall (%)
Traditional	36	48	42
Moderate	44	38	41
Progressive	20	15	17

Source: CARA Bishop Survey, 2016.

Who Is the Average Bishop?

The average bishop in the United States is 65 years old and has served for 12 years in a diocese not in his home state or region. He is a non-Hispanic white, born in the United States. He graduated from a Catholic high school, went to a college seminary after high school, and earned a graduate degree in theology. Prior to being named a bishop, he served as both an associate pastor and then pastor of a parish and also spent several years in an administrative role in the diocese. As a bishop he leads a diocese of about 250,000 Catholics in 92 parishes served by 87 active diocesan priests (another 51 diocesan priests are retired, infirm, or serving in other dioceses) and 98 permanent deacons. His diocese has about 250 sisters, but most of them are retired. Depending on the geographic location of the diocese, the bishop is challenged by either a stable or diminishing Catholic population or rapid growth and diversity.

Profile of Bishops over Time

Using a dataset that includes all Latin Rite ordinaries active between 1978 and 2017, Table 1.7 displays the characteristics of bishops appointed as the ordinary of a diocese during four different time papacies (the lengthy reign of Pope John Paul II is divided into two time periods). Throughout this 40-year period, the bishops are predominantly Caucasian and U.S. born. Pope Benedict XVI was more likely to appoint Hispanic bishops. During the earlier period of his pontificate, Pope John Paul II was more likely

Table 1.7 Bishop Characteristics over Time by Pope that Appointed Them[a]

Characteristic	Paul VI 1963–1978 (%)	John Paul II 1978–1991 (%)	John Paul II 1992–2005 (%)	Benedict XVI 2005–2013 (%)	Francis 2013–2017 (%)
Race					
White	97	92	89	87	89
African-American	1	2	5	0	5
Hispanic	2	5	7	12	5
Asian-Pacific	0	0	0	1	2
Native American	0	2	0	0	0
Religious order	2	15	9	8	9
US-born	96	98	95	91	96
Prior auxiliary	59	61	60	40	43
Graduate degree (beyond seminary)					
None	34	31	20	22	36
Canon law	26	18	22	31	28
Theology	33	37	39	39	46
Professional	17	17	20	19	10
Other	9	21	12	12	7
Studied in Rome	33	38	40	42	44
Total N	125	122	123	78	44

[a] An additional 32 bishops appointed by Pope Pius XII or Pope John XXIII were active ordinaries during this time period, but are not included in this table.

Source: Hoegeman Bishop Information Database, 1978–2017.

to have appointed members of religious orders. Ordinaries appointed by Pope Benedict XVI and Pope Francis were less likely to have had prior experience as an auxiliary. Those appointed during the latter part of Pope John Paul II's pontificate and by Pope Benedict XVI were more likely to have graduate degrees beyond the standard seminary education. Early Pope John Paul II appointees were more likely to have a graduate degree in a traditional academic field (a subject other than canon law, theology, or a professional field such as psychology, social work, or education). There are no significant differences among popes regarding whether or not an appointee studied in Rome.

The next chapter will explore how the bishops manage the many challenges of their diocese in their day-to-day schedule. What are they doing each day?

2

A Day in the Life of a Bishop

*People were coming and going in great numbers, and they
had no opportunity even to eat.*

MARK 6:31

*The responsibilities never stop. There's never a tiny pause,
any day of the year.*

BISHOP FROM A DIOCESE IN THE NORTHEAST

THIS CHAPTER DESCRIBES a "typical" day in the very busy lives of the 178
Latin Rite ordinaries serving in the United States, from the moment they
wake up in the morning until they say their final prayers before retiring at
night. We follow them through their liturgical celebrations, pastoral visits,
and administrative meetings, and even their physical exercise routines
and media preferences for their daily intake of news.

For each human being, every day is different. It is impossible to describe a
perfectly "normal" day, since no two are exactly alike, but we all spend our 24
hours every day doing much of the same things: sleeping, eating, drinking,
commuting, working, attending meetings, exercising, catching up on the
news, and taking care of our various personal and familial needs. Bishops
have the same 24 hours that everyone else has. Most lay Catholics, however,
have little idea how bishops spend their time on a normal day, as they only
see them on special occasions, such as at a Confirmation ceremony or during
a parish visitation.

So how do bishops spend their time each day? And how do they compare with the general population? Do they work longer or shorter hours
than most other people? Do they sleep more or less than people their age?
We make all comparisons with the general public using the most recent
data from the Bureau of Labor Statistics (BLS), a subdivision of the United

States Department of Labor.[1] Given that the average age of bishops is 65, we compare them to American adult males in that same age category.

Sleeping

We begin with the activity that occupies about a third of each day for most human beings. According to the BLS, the average American male between the ages of 55 and 64 sleeps 8.3 hours a day, while those aged 65 and older sleep an average of 8.9 hours a day. Since the average age of bishops falls right on the cusp of these two categories, we take the midpoint of 8.6 hours as our point of comparison. Bishops report sleeping an average of only 6.5 hours per night, which is 2.1 hours (24 percent) less than the average per day. Over the course of a year, this difference in the amount of sleep adds up to 767 hours, which is the equivalent to 31.9 full days. So by shaving off 2.1 hours of sleep a day, bishops gain a whole month of "awake" time per year. According to a report citing the National Health Interview Survey, lawyers, doctors, and social workers all sleep an average of seven hours a night.[2]

Figure 2.1 shows that 40 percent of bishops sleep seven hours a night, the minimum recommended by the National Sleep Foundation[3] for men in their age bracket. Only one bishop reported getting nine hours, which is the high end of the range recommended by the same foundation. As stated above, the average number of hours spent sleeping is 6.5. Twelve percent get less than six hours. A third (34 percent) get between 6 and 6.5 hours, and 13 percent sleep at least 7.5 hours a night.

Like many other people who feel the weight of their serious responsibilities, the bishops deprive themselves of sleep to have more time for work, which for many of them never seems to end. However, work is not the first activity they engage in at the beginning of the day. Most prefer

---

1. Bureau of Labor Statistics, U.S. Department of Labor, *American Time Use Survey*, https://www.bls.gov/tus/.

2. Debra Cassens Weiss, "Law is Second-Most Sleep-Deprived Profession, Federal Survey Finds," *ABA Journal*, February 27, 2012, http://www.abajournal.com/news/article/law_is_second-most_sleep_deprived_profession_federal_survey_finds/.

3. Max Hirshkowitz, Kaitlyn Whiton, Steven M. Albert, Cathy Alessi, Oliviero Bruni, Lydia DonCarlos . . . Paula J. Adams Hillard, "National Sleep Foundation's Sleep Time Duration Recommendations: Methodology and Results Summary," *Sleep Health* 1, no. 1 (2015). http://www.sleephealthjournal.org/article/S2352-7218%2815%2900015-7/fulltext.

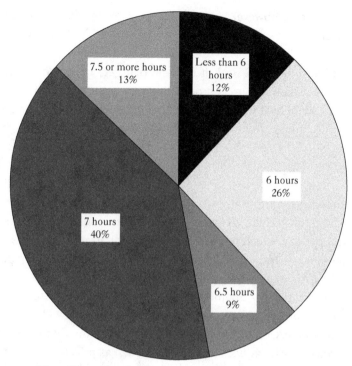

FIGURE 2.1 Time Spent Sleeping
Source: CARA Bishop Survey, 2016.

to rise early to have quiet time to pray, to be alone with God, before their other daily activities begin.

A bishop from a midsize western diocese said:

> I usually get up at 5:30 or 6:00 in the morning. I like to spend my prayer time in the chapel for about 45 minutes in the morning. After that, if I don't have a public Mass to celebrate later in the day, I will say Mass in my own chapel. After that I have breakfast, read the newspaper, and then get to the office by 9 o'clock.

A bishop from a large southern diocese reported a similar pattern:

> I get up around 6:00 and what I do immediately is have a cup of coffee and read the paper and then spend quality time in prayer. That's my major prayer time.

Not all bishops, however, are early risers. A bishop from a smaller diocese reports:

> I don't like mornings. So I'm not one that gets up at 4:00, 5:00, or 6:00. I usually get up at 7:00. I live very close to the office and I have to be there at 9:00, so generally I get up in the morning and I pray.

Praying

In the interviews, almost all bishops reported prayer as being their first major activity of the day. They pray an average of 108 minutes (almost two hours) per day, which includes time for meditation, Mass, the Divine Office, the Rosary, and other devotions. The shortest amount of reported daily prayer time was 45 minutes by one bishop, and the longest was six hours (720 minutes) by another. The most frequent response, given by two out of five bishops (39 percent), was that they pray two hours a day. It would be interesting to compare the amount of time that the bishops spend in prayer each day with that of others such as priests, religious, and laity. Sadly, no reliable comparative data are available at this time.

Most bishops pray early in the day, before they get caught up in an ongoing series of meetings, office work, and public events. A bishop from a western diocese said:

> I usually say Vespers in the evening. Everything else I try to pray early in the morning as I mentioned before. Once in a while, I like to pray the Rosary by walking around the park that's near where I live. I really enjoy that. I put on my ear phones and walk around listening to the Divine Office being chanted by some monks in Europe or just praying the Rosary as I walk. I find it very consoling and relaxing.

A busy bishop, who is on many national boards and is very active, both at the USCCB and at his state's episcopal conference, said:

> My goal is to spend anywhere from 45 minutes to an hour in prayer every day. Sometimes that's realized, and sometimes it's not. But, my goal is 45 minutes a day in personal prayer, contemplative prayer. I try to do most of it in the morning, and then in the evening,

shorter periods. But I also drive myself everywhere so very often if I am out of town on the way back home in the car, I also use that time for prayer.

An auxiliary bishop, who is also pastor of a large suburban parish, mentioned:

I aim at four 15-minute intervals of prayer a day. But one of my main times to pray is from 2:00 to 3:00 in the morning as it is the quietest time of the day. I just wake up then [without the aid of an alarm clock] and pray usually for 15 to 30 minutes, sometimes up to an hour, and then I am able to go right back to sleep.

Exercising

Two-thirds of the Latin Rite ordinaries report engaging in some form of physical exercise every day. While a full third (34 percent) say that they do not exercise at all on a normal day, another third gets between 15 and 30 minutes a day, and the last third gets between 45 minutes and two hours a day. The Latin Rite auxiliaries and the retired bishops follow a similar pattern. However, of the 11 Eastern Rite eparchs responding to the question, six (55 percent) report getting in an hour of exercise every day. Another three (27 percent) report exercising for half an hour a day and only two (18 percent) report no exercise on a daily basis.

Besides workout routines, one bishop mentioned two other forms of exercise that he finds relaxing:

I like to play a round of golf once in a while, and the Irish priests love to golf. We will get out to play. There is a difference with retired priests because the jurisdiction is very different. I find I can relax a little more with them and that has been good. The other part is I brought my dog with me. Fortunately, there is a couple that takes him every day when I come to the office or when overnight or on vacation—so he is in good hands. I've had the animal for ten years and that is a big support. I think anybody who has a pet will understand that. My health has been good. I'm 66 . . . and fortunately, having taken care of myself through the years, I don't find any issue yet that prevents me from being very active. Thank God for that.

Reading or Watching the News

Many bishops spend some time in the morning reading the newspaper or watching the news on television before they get to their offices. This activity is often done as part of their breakfast routine. Many of them also watch the news at the end of their busy days before going to sleep. Figure 2.2 shows how much time bishops spend informing themselves with news. On average, they spend a total of 78 minutes a day in this activity. While 8 percent report not reading newspapers or watching TV news on a daily basis, more than half (53 percent) report spending between 30 and 60 minutes on these activities every day. Slightly more than a third (34 percent) report spending one and a half to two hours a day in news consumption. Only 5 percent said that they spend three hours or more on this activity.

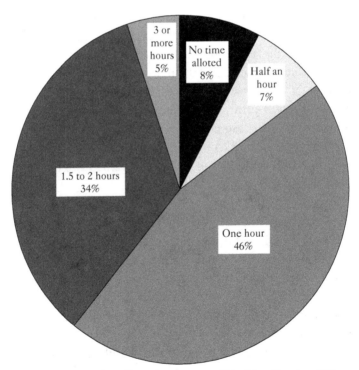

FIGURE 2.2 Time Spent Reading Newspaper or Watching News on TV
Source: CARA Bishop Survey, 2016.

What Secular Newspapers Do They Read?

Figure 2.3 displays the bishops' preferred printed secular news sources. Almost nine out of ten (88 percent) reported getting their printed news via their local newspaper. The next most popular daily source for them is *The New York Times* (38 percent) followed by *The Wall Street Journal* (24 percent) and *USA Today* (23 percent). Only 6 percent read *The Washington Post*. Theologically progressive bishops (65 percent) are more likely than either moderate (38 percent) or traditional (27 percent) bishops to read *The New York Times*. None of this is particularly surprising. (The total cumulative percentage of responses is higher than 100 percent because they were allowed to mention more than one newspaper. Obviously, many of them read more than one.)

What Religious Newspapers Do They Read?

On the other hand, it is interesting to note their sources for Church news. Figure 2.4 shows these results. At the head of the list (61 percent) is the

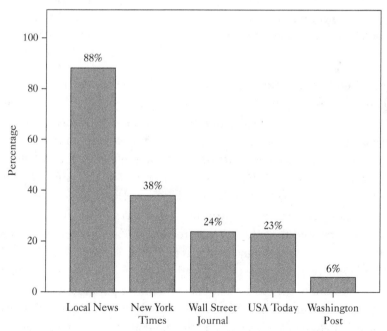

FIGURE 2.3 Secular Newspapers Read
Source: CARA Bishop Survey, 2016.

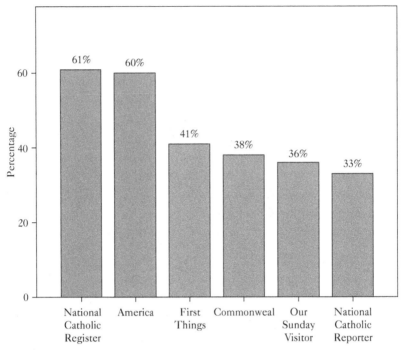

FIGURE 2.4 Religious News Sources
Source: CARA Bishop Survey, 2016.

National Catholic Register, which is owned and operated by Eternal Word Television Network (EWTN), and which definitely leans in the traditional direction, as compared to the last-place finisher, the *National Catholic Reporter* (33 percent), which has a much more progressive slant. A reversal in ideological emphasis is expressed in their preference for the liberal, Jesuit-run *America* magazine (60 percent) over *First Things* (41 percent), which was founded by the late Reverend Richard Neuhaus, a conservative convert priest. The progressive-leaning *Commonweal* is read by 38 percent of the bishops, and the middle-of-the-road *Our Sunday Visitor* by 36 percent. Two bishops wrote in by hand that they read *The Tablet* and *Inside the Vatican.* Only one bishop reported reading *The Wanderer,* considered by many to be among the most traditional of Catholic publications.

Statistically significant differences surfaced upon analysis of the theological orientation of the bishops and the religious news sources they read. Almost three-fourths (73 percent) of the traditionally-minded bishops reported reading the *National Catholic Register,* whereas only four out of ten (40 percent) of the progressive bishops did, with the moderates

(59 percent) falling in between. Analyzing the readership of the *National Catholic Reporter* showed the opposite results. Only one-quarter (25 percent) of the traditional and moderate bishops read that publication, in contrast to seven in ten (70 percent) of the progressive bishops.

The contrast between traditional and progressive is even greater when analyzing the readership of *America* magazine. Only one-third (32 percent) of the traditional bishops read this national publication, in contrast to the vast majority (95 percent) of the progressive bishops. In this case, moderates are closer to the progressives at 75 percent. *Commonweal* magazine has a similar spread, with an 18 percent versus 75 percent readership contrast between the more traditional and the progressive bishops, respectively, with the moderates right in between at 43 percent. Figure 2.5 shows this stark divergence.

What Television Channels Do They Watch?

Among the TV cable news channels in the United States today, FOX is the more conservative station, while MSNBC is the more liberal one. CNN is usually considered middle-of-the-road. Given the overall traditional

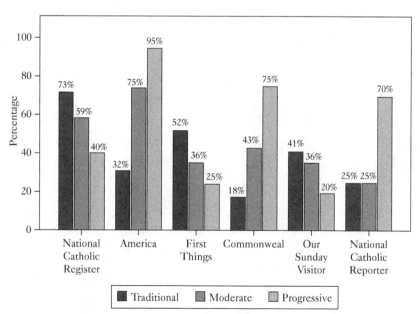

FIGURE 2.5 Religious News Sources by Theological Orientation
Source: CARA Bishop Survey, 2016.

leaning of the bishops, it is no surprise that so few of them tuned in to MSNBC for their news. While it is hard to obtain reliable data for national viewership, according to *USA Today*,[4] and based on Nielsen ratings, FOX News is ranked number one in the nation in 2016 with a viewership of 2.844 million compared to 1.164 million for CNN and 1.160 million for MSNBC.

Figure 2.6 shows bishops' choices for TV news. Almost half of the bishops (47 percent) reported they watch the news on the FOX Network. A third (35 percent) get their news from CNN. These two cable companies are much more popular with the bishops than the three major networks (ABC, CBS, and NBC). MSNBC came in last place with 4 percent. Many bishops listed more than one station as their source for news.

When analyzing theological orientation and TV news viewership, there is no statistically significant difference among any of the channels, except for FOX. Two-thirds (68 percent) of the traditionally-minded bishops watched FOX compared to 40 percent of moderates, and only 11 percent of the progressive bishops.

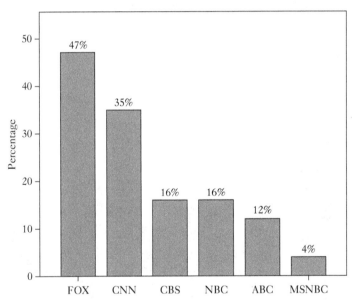

FIGURE 2.6 Source of TV News
Source: CARA Bishop Survey, 2016.

---

4. Mike Snider, "Cable News Ratings Drop Post-Election," *USA Today*, February 1, 2017, US edition, https://www.pressreader.com/usa/usa-today-us-edition/20170201/281556585554558.

Working

Like most men their age who are still active in the work force, bishops spend most of their waking hours working. Their work hours can be divided into three main categories: (1) working in office, (2) attending meetings, and (3) attending functions. Overall, bishops reported working 9.8 hours a day on average: 4.5 hours in their offices, 3.4 hours attending meetings, and 1.9 hours attending events.

According to the BLS, the average employed American male between the ages of 55 and 64 works 8.1 hours a day, while the average employed American male over 65 works 7.1 hours a day.[5] As we did with the comparison of the amount of time spent sleeping, we take the midpoint (7.6 hours) between the two groups as our point of comparison. This means that bishops work about 2.2 hours (29 percent) more per day than their peers. Recall that the bishops sleep 2.1 hours less than their counterparts, so it would seem that the time that they shave off from sleeping is spent working.

A bishop, who has requested that the pope appoint an auxiliary bishop to help him because he is feeling overwhelmed by so many responsibilities, reports:

> I'm pretty much at the office the whole day, from 9 in the morning until 5 p.m., between meetings and other work in the office. Almost every evening, there's some event such as a banquet I must attend, or a meeting with benefactors, or a Confirmation celebration in a parish. I try to get home early and like to go to bed by 10 o'clock.

Another solo bishop, but one who does not want an auxiliary, says:

> I head to the office at 9. I usually have Mass to celebrate somewhere [at a school or a parish]. Mass is not always at the same time. Mass is sometimes private, and there are appointments throughout the day. I don't have a cook so in the evening I go back to my house. During the day, I stay in the office, or I'm out on the road. I have evening celebrations— things like that. I'm not one to end my day busy. You know, I can't have a Confirmation that ends at 9 o'clock and then go

---

5. Bureau of Labor Statistics, *American Time Use Survey.*

home and go to bed right away. I need time to transition. I'll pray at
the end of the day, so I'm usually up until 11 or midnight.

An extremely busy archbishop, who has an auxiliary bishop but is still
stretched thin in many different directions, states:

By 8:30 or 9:00 [in the morning] I either go over to the office, or
have ceremonies at schools or parishes, or special events. So, in
the morning, it would either be appointments or ceremonies. The
same in the afternoon or on any given weekend, it is usually at least
10 to 12 events or even more in any given week. So that takes me out
of the office, but I also spend a lot of time in the office for appointments with staff as well as with people from the outside. I never
refuse an appointment, if someone wants to see me. I never refuse
an appointment with staff or anyone. I am also very attentive to responding to mail. No letter goes unanswered, and of course, almost
every night, there is a ceremony or a meeting. I am on an incredible
number of boards and committees and that takes a lot of time. . . .
I normally go to bed between 11 and 12. If I get home in the evening
after a ceremony, I watch the news, have a glass of wine, and spend
some more time in prayer.

An auxiliary bishop from a large archdiocese, who is also the pastor of
a large suburban parish, owes his ability to fulfill all his episcopal duties to
the parochial vicars who serve at his parish. He states:

The responsibilities never stop. There's never a tiny pause, any day
of the year. . . . The huge advantage that I have had over the years is
that I have had very qualified associates (parochial vicars) who will
take care of anything and who are *de facto* administrators. . . . They
have accepted the challenge of working with me. The added responsibilities were good for them because they were very capable of per-
forming them. The quality of these priests is the biggest advantage
I have. . . . Sometimes Fr. N. [the current parochial vicar] will take
the early morning Mass, if I have other responsibilities, and I don't
get back until late at night. Often, there will be a note on my door
that someone else will cover the early Mass, which was assigned to
me, which is outstanding.

Number of Days Working

The bishops reported working an average of 6.3 days a week. Half of them (49 percent) said that they work six days, and a third (33 percent) work seven days a week. One in eight (12 percent) work 6.5 days, and only 4 percent reported less than six days a week. If we multiply the average of 9.8 work hours a day by the average of 6.3 days a week, the total number of hours bishops work per week comes to 61.7. We also asked a separate question about how many hours they work a week. The average response to that item was 63.2 hours. If we take the average of these two responses, we can estimate that bishops work about 62.5 hours a week. Carroll[6] reported that Catholic priests work an average of 56 hours per week, which means that bishops work roughly 6.5 hours (12 percent) more per week than priests do. Those extra hours per week add up to 338 more hours per year, which is the equivalent to 14 full 24-hour days over the course of one year.

One of the main roles that sets bishops apart from priests is that they are usually the ones to administer the Sacrament of Confirmation in their diocese. In some cases, bishops may delegate this faculty to priests, but that is an exception to the rule. The bishops in this study averaged 38 Confirmation ceremonies a year, and 36 parish visitations that were not part of a Confirmation ceremony. That comes to about three Confirmation ceremonies and three parish visitations per month. There is a wide range of responses: from one bishop who presides at only six Confirmation ceremonies in a year to one who does so 100 times, which would average two every week. Similarly, parish visitations fluctuated from five to 133 a year, meaning that a particular bishop on the high end of the spectrum visits, on average, two and a half parishes a week. Confirmations can be scheduled on any day of the week, but most parish visitations occur on a weekend when the vast majority of the parishioners can attend. A parish visitation can also coincide with the installation of a new pastor by the bishop. It is on these two kinds of occasions that the majority of lay Catholics get to meet their bishop in person.

Besides making the rounds of the parishes in their dioceses, which for bishops in rural areas may entail long hours of driving, many bishops also travel outside their diocese for various reasons. On average, they are out

---

6. Jackson W. Carroll, *God's Potters: Pastoral Leadership and the Shaping of Congregations* (Grand Rapids, MI: William B. Eerdmans, 2006).

of their diocese 3.9 days a month. The range of answers to this question was extremely wide, from zero to 25 days a month. The most common answers were three days (23 percent), two days (21 percent), four days (14 percent), and five days (12 percent). We did not ask them to specify what they did when they were away. Three typical reasons would be to attend a USCCB committee meeting, to give a talk or to participate in a conference in another diocese, or to attend a meeting of a national board on which they serve.

Perhaps they also use some of their days away just to rest. On average, the bishops reported taking three weeks of vacation a year. A third (35 percent) reported taking two weeks or less. Another third (35 percent) took exactly three weeks, and one in six (18 percent) reported getting between 3.5 and 5 weeks.

In conclusion, we have seen that the average Catholic bishop in the United States today is quite the workaholic, sacrificing on average two hours of sleep a night in order to keep up with all of his responsibilities. As we will see in the next chapter, part of the reason why he may work such long hours is because he derives great satisfaction from his ministry.

3

Satisfactions in Episcopal Life and Ministry

I am happy as a bishop. I never imagined this coming but a lot of grace is part of it too.

BISHOP FROM A SOUTHERN DIOCESE

For me the sacred role, the liturgical role, is the most important—to bring people into the presence of God and to help people be brought into an experience where they can come to know and love Jesus. That to me is my most important role and that's the role from which I derive the most satisfaction. For example, when I officiate at a Confirmation, I find that is a key moment where I can do precisely that.

BISHOP FROM A WESTERN DIOCESE

IN SPITE OF the demanding schedules and the long days described in Chapter 2, overall the bishops reported remarkably high levels of satisfaction. They take seriously their vocations as "successors to the Apostles," and they feel the weight of the responsibilities placed upon their shoulders in an increasingly secularized and seemingly post-Christian era. However, as this chapter demonstrates, they do not allow those daily burdens and their concomitant frustrations to stifle their contentment. Chapter 4 focuses on the specific problems and challenges that the bishops experience, but in this chapter we first explore the "bright" side, the various components and sources of bishops' satisfaction. When possible, we compare their responses to those made by priests in the most recent national study of priests described in *Same Call, Different Men.*[1]

---

1. Mary L. Gautier, Paul M. Perl, and Stephen J. Fichter, *Same Call, Different Men: The Evolution of the Priesthood since Vatican II* (Collegeville, MN: Liturgical Press, 2012).

Usually when the two words *bishop* and *satisfaction* are placed in the same sentence, they refer to one of two things. It could mean priests' satisfaction with their bishop's leadership style, which Rossetti (2011) has shown to be the number one contributing factor in priests' overall contentment.[2] It could also mean the laity's approval rating of the bishops, which a Pew Research study has shown to have risen from only 51 percent during the heat of the 2002 priest sex-abuse scandal to 70 percent ten years later.[3] Clearly, the bishops have recouped some of the loss of credibility in their leadership. Even though both these topics are important, this chapter does not deal with either one of them, but rather looks at the experiences of the bishops themselves to see what makes them happy and what brings them satisfaction and, to some extent, what causes them frustration.

In response to the survey question "I am satisfied with my life as a bishop," more than three out of five (63 percent) agreed "strongly" and a full third (34 percent) agreed "somewhat" with that statement, for an overall combined 97 percent satisfaction rate. Only three bishops (2 percent) disagreed "somewhat" and one bishop (0.8 percent) disagreed "strongly." While these satisfaction rates are extremely high, they are not completely surprising. A National Opinion Research Center (NORC) study revealed that clergy exhibit higher levels of satisfaction than any other occupation.[4] Less than half (47 percent) of the general population in this NORC study described themselves as "very satisfied" with their work, whereas the overwhelming majority (87 percent) of clergy reported the same.

Keeping in mind that only 9 percent of Latin Rite ordinaries live in the diocese where they were raised, it is remarkable that 90 percent of them say that they feel their current diocese is their home. While the small numbers limit testing for statistical significance, it is worth mentioning that all four bishops (3.2 percent) who reported some level of overall dissatisfaction

2. Stephen Rossetti, *Why Priests Are Happy: A Study of the Psychological and Spiritual Health of Priests* (Notre Dame, IN: Ave Maria Press, 2011).

3. Russell Heimlich, "Most U.S. Catholics Say They are Satisfied with the Leadership Provided by U.S. Nuns and Sisters," Pew Research Center, August 6, 2012, http://www.pewresearch.org/fact-tank/2012/08/06/most-u-s-catholics-say-they-are-satisfied-with-the-leadership-provided-by-u-s-nuns-and-sisters/.

4. University of Chicago News Office, "Looking for Satisfaction and Happiness in a Career? Start by Choosing a Job that Helps Others," April 17, 2007, http://www-news.uchicago.edu/releases/07/070417.jobs.shtml.

currently live outside their diocese of origin. Conversely, all 11 bishops who reside in their home diocese expressed satisfaction.

Since priests are the bishops' closest collaborators, it makes sense that feeling accepted by the majority of their priests would be a major contributing factor to these high rates of episcopal satisfaction. Only one Latin Rite ordinary reported not feeling accepted by the majority of his priests. This means that literally 99 percent of the bishops who participated in our survey felt accepted by the majority of their priests. Whether or not this feeling of acceptance reported by the bishops corresponds to the actual acceptance rates by the priests of their dioceses is a question worthy of inspection but is outside the realm of our current study.

A bishop from the southern part of the United States spoke of the positive relationship that he has with the majority of the priests whose ministry he supervises:

> The vast majority is very cooperative. Rarely when I am doing assignments would someone say "no" or "I'll think about it." In general, I find them extremely supportive. I find them extremely collaborative and very fraternal. With some regularity, they come to me with issues or problems and ask my advice. That's the vast majority.

A very busy bishop from the Northeast, who served in parish ministry for many years, said this about his relationship with the priests under his care:

> I have the advantage of having been in their situation. I understand, so when they tell me their story I understand it and know they are not making it up. People's greatest need is to feel understood so I try to take the time and listen to them and make them feel understood. In half the cases, they can solve the problem themselves, and with mature healthy adults, this builds strong relationships. With the majority of priests, I have a strong healthy relationship.

Many sociological studies explore response variation related to age, race, ethnicity, and various socioeconomic variables. We did not find any subgroup variation in satisfaction levels among the bishops based on these standard demographic categories, nor based on whether or not they belong to a religious order, which we hypothesized might be a factor. Obviously, there was no need to analyze gender differences since all Catholic bishops are male.

As might be expected from such highly satisfied men, 80 percent reported no major problem with burnout. Only 17 percent said that they agreed "somewhat" to feeling burned out frequently, while the remaining 3 percent "strongly" agreed. However, this low level of burnout (or high level of satisfaction) does not mean that they always perform the kind of duties they prefer. When asked if they would be happier if they dedicated more time to pastoral activity rather than administrative tasks, nearly seven out of ten (69 percent) agreed. Along these same lines, 83 percent reported wishing they could spend more time with the priests of their diocese. Sixty percent said they wished they had more time to be available to counsel all the priests under their care, and 56 percent felt that they were often too busy to pray as much as they would like.

Time is definitely at a premium in their busy lives, but clearly, bishops are happy in their ministry. A 74-year-old bishop, just one year away from retirement, described this mixture of intense and frenetic activity with the immense joy and satisfaction that he derives from it:

> When I go around for Confirmations, which are almost 70 a year, not counting installations of new pastors or celebrations of the anniversaries of parishes, I can be out six nights in a row and have had five Confirmations in a weekend at three different churches. I can only concentrate on one at a time and cross that hurdle and go on to the next one. It requires quite a bit of energy and focus. . . . The responsibilities never stop. There's never a tiny pause, any day of the year. I don't think unless you work in my office you would ever know that. When you start to do the math, you see how much work there is. We have close to 80 parishes with almost 180 priests. . . . Just the number of pastors who have to be installed, the interviews of guys finishing their terms or joining the pastors' pool, the number of complaints that come in on a daily basis. It's a full time job.

Given the immense amount of responsibility that each of them has, it will be helpful to know from what sources they derive such high levels of satisfaction. Table 3.1 compares the responses given by the bishops in this study to the responses of the priests who participated in the study published in *Same Call, Different Men.*[5]

As Table 3.1 clearly demonstrates, the bishops reported even higher rates of satisfaction than the priests across the board, with the only exception being the respect that comes from the priestly/episcopal office. We did not expect the sources of satisfaction to follow the exact order from highest to lowest for both bishops and priests. This makes sense, however, since bishops are simply priests who have been chosen by the pope to exercise oversight in the local church. Nor did we expect the bishops to report such consistently higher levels of satisfaction than priests do.

Table 3.1 Comparing Sources of Satisfaction between Bishops and Priests

"How important is each of the following as a source of satisfaction to you?"	"Great" importance		
	Bishops (%)	Priests (%)	Difference (%)
Joy of administering the sacraments and presiding over the liturgy	97	94	+3
Satisfaction of preaching the Word	89	83	+6
Being part of a community of Christians who are working together to share the Good News of the Gospel	84	73	+11
Opportunity to work with many people and be a part of their lives	77	71	+6
Serving as an *alter Christus* to the faithful	73	54	+19
Challenge of being the leader of a Catholic Christian community	62	50	+12
Organizing and administering the work of the Church	43	30	+13
Engaging in efforts at social reform	38	25	+13
Respect that comes to the priestly/episcopal office	7	22	−15

Source: CARA Bishop Survey, 2016; Gautier et al., 2012.

---

5. Gautier et al., *Same Call, Different Men.*

Joy of Administering the Sacraments, Presiding over the Liturgy, and Preaching the Word

Almost all the bishops (97 percent) cited their sacramental and liturgical role as the source of their greatest satisfaction, which was similar to the priests' very high response (94 percent). During our interviews, the bishops consistently spoke about the joy they derive from fulfilling these episcopal functions, with special emphasis on conferring the sacrament of Confirmation. As we stated previously, most lay Catholics only meet their bishops at a Confirmation ceremony, their own or that of a relative or friend. This particular point of encounter is a moment that most bishops cherish.

A bishop from a Midwestern diocese, who had previously served as an auxiliary in a much larger archdiocese, said:

> I just love doing Confirmations. Ours is eighth, ninth, and tenth grade, and so it requires a lot of flexibility. It is a great opportunity to be with these young people. I know there is a great problem of the fall off of the young people after Confirmation. I just like to think that this is a good experience for them. Now we have to figure out some way to tap more into that experience to make it more enduring, and I know everybody is struggling with that . . . [I find it most consoling] when I'm doing Confirmation or celebrating a big Mass like Christmas Mass or ordinations. Gathering the people together and leading worship with them, I find that very, very enjoyable. We have an annual convocation of our priests and a pretty good turnout for that, and I always enjoyed that great gathering. I tend to be kind of a people person, so I like to be with people.

A bishop who confirms hundreds of young people every year shared a specific memory that clearly touched his heart:

> I get overwhelmingly positive responses to my homilies at Confirmations almost everywhere I go, and people tell me how much it meant to them. I received a startling three-page letter from a 12-year-old girl, who was probably the youngest person I confirmed, and it was very touching. She said how much what

I said during the Confirmation meant to her and said she wanted this to be a conversion point for her life and that I enabled that to happen by explaining to her the role of responsibility in her growing up.

Another bishop was actually not very keen on Confirmation ceremonies, although he loved leading liturgies:

> I get a great amount of satisfaction from my liturgical role. I really enjoy special services, special occasions, and the liturgical year in general. Not so much Confirmations. They are not a big deal to me. You don't see your people. Most of the sponsors are from outside your diocese or parish. I would say it is more anniversaries of parishes, your Christmas and Easter Masses, the Rite of Election at the Cathedral, the Chrism Mass, anniversaries, etc. I am a people person, and I enjoy being with the people even after the service. I always liked having a reception after the major celebrations.

In second place, after the joy of administering the sacraments, nearly nine out of ten (89 percent) bishops (and 83 percent of priests) say that they derive "great" satisfaction from "preaching the Word." An archbishop from a very diverse diocese with large swaths of rural areas spoke about his effort to get out to the faraway parishes on a regular basis to preach and to teach:

> It's easy to get to the city parishes, but it takes effort and scheduling to get to the rural parishes, but I do that pretty regularly. I like to be present, and I've been here almost eight years, so I appreciate the fact that I know a lot of people by name. We sort of know where they fit, what community they are a part of. As soon as I get there, I catch up pretty quickly on who they are and what they're up to. . . . I'm not just there to be visiting, but by my presence to encourage the local pastor and other pastoral leaders in their work. . . . Connected to that role is the role of teacher. In my own preaching and teaching, I try to be prepared so that what I say is both good in terms of its content and in terms of what people are thinking or asking about.

Community of Christians and Working with Many People

Another strong majority (84 percent of bishops compared to 73 percent of priests) stated that "being part of a community of Christians who are working together to share the Good News of the Gospel" is an important source of satisfaction for them. Closely linked to that is the "opportunity to work with many people and be part of their lives," which 77 percent of bishops described as a source of "great" satisfaction compared to 71 percent for the priests. A few quotes from the interviews illustrate this important point of community building. For example, two archbishops, who are in charge of two very large archdioceses, said:

> We have had to undertake a pastoral planning process. We have decided to root it firmly in evangelization, not just do a planning process and call it an evangelization process but to build it from the ground up. Based on mission, it's answering the question what does the mission require of us? How should we be present? How can we marshal our resources to do the mission most effectively? And we basically are rooting it in *Evangelii Gaudium* with Pope Francis as our guide. . . . It's a heavily consultative process, and it's across the board. I call it a synod on wheels.
>
> [I try to] create a culture of unity. We heard people talk about how fractured their lives are and how they feel even in the Church. While there's not a lot of hostility or lack of respect in the archdiocese, [in] a lot of ways, we are looking past each other [in terms of] cultures, languages, and generations. People are worried about the next generation of kids and their grandkids. So, another priority is to try to bring together the diverse gifts where we can, so that there can be a greater benefit to all of the diversity.

A bishop who is currently leading his diocese in the process of restructuring their mutual vision and pastoral priorities described his experience:

> So we have had 17 listening sessions that I was at. I sat there and listened to over eleven hundred people, two sessions with our priests, one with the Chancery staff, and then we had a team of fourteen, who met for seven days over three months, for six hours a day. All to put together the refreshed vision statement, mission statement,

and pastoral priorities. Well there is an awful lot of listening going on in that process, that is over most of the year. So I am blessed in that way. I am really seeing a new spirit and vision and mission emerging, and we are now ready to implement. We will gather back all the priests and all our lay ecclesial ministers . . . for two days, and we will look at specifically how we can do that. . . . [It is] an amazing way to lift up a diocese. It's great. That may be unique in terms of an opportunity to really work with folks and be at the center of an emerging new vision and renewed energy and all of that. It is good; it really is.

Serving as Alter Christus *and the Challenge of Being a Leader*

Three-quarters of bishops (as compared to just over half of priests) cited "serving as *alter Christus* to the faithful" as being a source of "great" satisfaction. Of all the differences in responses between the bishops and the priests, this 19-point variance is the largest. In *Same Call, Different Men,*[6] we discovered that the more conservative-minded (and usually younger) priests identified more with being "another Christ" than did their more progressive (and older) confreres.

As was the case with the priests, this particular source of satisfaction revealed statistically significant differences when comparing the responses of bishops according to their self-described theological orientation. Three-quarters (76 percent) of traditionally-minded bishops and 80 percent of moderate bishops cited "serving as *alter Christus*" as a source of "great" satisfaction compared to only half (50 percent) of the progressive bishops.

One possible explanation for the bishops apparently leaning in this more traditionalist direction is that Pope John Paul II and Pope Benedict XVI selected priests to be bishops from among the more conservative clergy. Under Pope Francis this trend seems to be shifting in the opposite direction, as explained by John Allen's reflection on Pope Francis'choice for the newest American cardinals.[7]

---

6. Ibid.

7. John Allen, "With Pope's Cardinal Picks, Bernardin's 'Seamless Garment' Is Back," *Crux*, October 9, 2016, https://cruxnow.com/analysis/2016/10/09/popes-cardinal-picks-bernardins-seamless-garment-back/.

The next strongest source of satisfaction for the bishops is the challenge of being a leader of a Catholic Christian community. An archbishop, who is very active in both the state bishop conference and with the USCCB, stated that his most important role as bishop is:

> To be a spiritual leader . . . a shepherd . . . not administration, not meetings, but the role of being the shepherd, the leader, the one that can work with the people, either individually or as a group on spiritual matters and on developing spirituality.

These are indeed challenging times to be a leader in the Catholic Church. Much work needs to be done both inside and out. As explained in *Catholic Parishes of the 21st Century*,[8] there are basically two different ecclesial realities in the United States today. For those who live within the large rectangle from Minneapolis to Saint Louis and then over to Baltimore and up to Boston (the Midwest and Northeast) there is a distinct feeling that the Church is shrinking or even withering. Hundreds of parishes and Catholic schools have closed; others have only survived through mergers. The Catholic population has shifted away from this area down to the South and out to the West, where the bishops cannot build churches and schools quickly enough. Whether concentrating on downsizing or on building, these shifting demographics mean that the bishops must dedicate much of their time to organizational and administrative tasks.

Organizing and Administering the Work of the Church

For 43 percent of bishops and 30 percent of priests, "organizing and administering the work of the Church" is a source of "great" satisfaction. Of the nine possible sources of satisfaction, this item is the first to dip below the 50 percent level. From the interviews, it seems that for many bishops administrative work is seen as an undesirable but necessary part of their job. A relatively new bishop spoke in these terms:

---

8. Charles E. Zech, Mary L. Gautier, Mark M. Gray, Jonathon L. Wiggins, and Thomas P. Gaunt, *Catholic Parishes of the 21st Century* (New York, NY: Oxford University Press, 2017).

I try to take care of the administrative tasks, and I know I have to be an effective collaborator with the heads of our various departments. They help me to stay balanced, but for me, the most important role is the sacred role—the liturgical role.

Many bishops described their administrative work in the context of a balancing act, as did this archbishop, who not only has to take care of his large archdiocese but is also involved in many national organizations and with the USCCB:

It's difficult to do. I think the most important [thing] is to be out and about among the people and to celebrate liturgies with them. I always try to do that for special events in the community. I always give that priority and rarely say no to an invitation. So I think that's the priority, and the second thing would be the administrative, but you can do that whenever. Wait. No. I think the second would be meeting people who ask for an appointment, people who are troubled and needing some direction. And the third would be the administration. Some days it's just very difficult to balance all of that.

Some felt unprepared for the administrative work that comes "with the job," as did this ordinary, who belongs to a religious order:

I did not feel prepared administratively. I never served as a vicar general or as an auxiliary bishop. Nor did I ever occupy any major chancery position. I never served as superior in my religious order. In essence, I was severely lacking in administrative experience. I have to admit that I have found that part of the job overwhelming. Otherwise, I felt prepared in many other ways. . . . I felt prepared spiritually and intellectually, but definitely not administratively.

A bishop from the Northeast felt that his previous assignments as vicar general in another diocese helped him to a degree but not entirely:

Being the vicar general and the moderator of the curia certainly exposes you to a diocesan-wide perspective. And it also introduces you to almost every issue that will come your way as a diocesan bishop. So in terms of the administrative experience that you gather, the role as vicar general and moderator of the curia was very, very helpful in some day becoming a diocesan bishop. On the other hand, there is nothing like having the final responsibility and final authority and everything does stop at your door and at your desk. So that is the part that is different. In terms of the experience and the issues, the challenges, and the problems that come your way as a bishop, certainly serving as vicar general and moderator of the curia was a very good preparation.

A bishop who had served as an auxiliary in a different diocese was very grateful that he had that administrative experience before he was assigned his own diocese:

> I'm very grateful that I was an auxiliary. I can't imagine going from being a pastor to being a bishop. That would blow my mind. I was an auxiliary for six years, and I very much appreciated those six years. I see the wisdom of serving as an auxiliary before being appointed a diocesan bishop. It's hard enough adjusting to life as a bishop in addition to have all this responsibility cast upon you when you are trying to . . . when your priesthood is taking off in a direction you never thought it would take. All of a sudden you are being asked to do something you never expected or wanted. But open to the Holy Spirit, you say yes. That's a lot of change from the focus of your life to being asked to do something that, at least as a pastor, I had never done before. That was chancery stuff . . . so as an auxiliary bishop, I was named vicar general and moderator of the curia. I didn't start that way. There was another auxiliary bishop serving in those roles. He became a bishop and those tasks fell to me. I am grateful for my time as an auxiliary bishop. I don't know how priests can go from being a pastor to being a bishop. I don't know how they do it, especially in a diocese you never served in.

An auxiliary bishop expressed admiration for his archbishop, who is the one who must take the bulk of the administrative load in their archdiocese. He tries to help where he can, but he feels as though his role of auxiliary limits his degree of participation:

> As an auxiliary bishop, I don't have the same central administrative responsibility as an archbishop has. For example, deciding

policy like what to do with our archdiocesan school system . . . that
is a very big decision. I happen to agree there is a need for some
centralization and oversight. Having capital campaigns to support
Catholic Charities are absolutely necessary. But they are tough decisions. The administrative decisions in an archdiocese are overwhelming . . . I am more of a consultant to [the archbishop and the
staff at the chancery] with regard to personnel. Parishioners don't
realize how big the archdiocese is. We have more than 1,100 build-
ings in the archdiocese. When I do Confirmations and go from an
all-Korean parish, to an all-Black one, to an all-Spanish one and to
an all-white one, you realize that the number of cultures interacting
within this archdiocese is amazing. It is a tremendous responsibility to be the archbishop in such a large archdiocese.

Engaging in Efforts at Social Reform

Over one-third (38 percent) of bishops (and 25 percent of priests) derive
"great" satisfaction from engaging in efforts at social reform. As with all
advocacy, frustration is part of the job description because of the polarized
nature of contemporary society.

In an interview, a bishop spoke about his efforts to engage the public
on the issues of environmental protection.

Our coastline is washing away. I wrote an op-ed piece for our local
newspaper. Basically, the position of my opinion piece was that we
have a moral responsibility to assist climate change refugees. That
was in a nutshell what I wrote about, and the paper printed my
opinion in its entirety. The paper then, a few days later, as they
sometimes do, had an opinion poll, and it said, "Do you agree
with the bishop that we have a moral obligation to assist climate
change refugees?" And I think 62 percent of the people said 'no'.
Now I don't know how many people responded; they only gave
percentages.

As with analyzing the *"alter Christus"* variable, satisfaction related to
efforts at social reform revealed statistically significant differences when
comparing the responses of bishops according to their theological orientation. Two-thirds (67 percent) of progressive bishops spoke about engagement in social reform as a source of "great" satisfaction, while only

one-fifth (20 percent) of traditionally-minded and almost half (48 percent) of moderate bishops reported the same level of satisfaction.

Respect that Comes to the Episcopal Office

As stated earlier, "respect that comes to the episcopal office" is a source of "great" satisfaction for just 7 percent of bishops, 15 percentage points lower than it is for priests. Given all the turmoil that came in the wake of the priest sexual abuse scandal and the anger that so many people vented toward the bishops, this is not a particularly surprising discovery.

One bishop stated he was afraid that when he became bishop his priests would treat him with a distanced "respect" which would mean the loss of friendship:

> in a very beautiful way . . . they respected my new position without distancing themselves from me. It was very beautiful to see that. When we would meet one on one, they still call me [by my nickname], but in public, they would say Bishop [last name]. They would recognize the role. I have to say I was worried about that . . . how are the priests going to treat me, because you know, "oh he's a bishop now . . . the furthest distance away the better" [laughs], but they didn't do that with me.

The only statistically significant geographic difference we found in terms of the analysis of these satisfaction variables came with this last one. None of the bishops from the Midwest and the Northeast mentioned deriving "great" satisfaction from "the respect that comes to the episcopal office," but 20 percent of the bishops from the South and four percent from the West did. None of our additional analyses explained this difference, but perhaps the higher proportion of Hispanics (who generally tend to be more deferential to authority figures) in the South and the West may be a factor.

A bishop from the South spoke about the respect that characterizes the interpersonal relationships among people in that part of the country:

> [Disrespect] is not a challenge here. I think it is in some other places, but it is not as big of a challenge here. Even if people disagree with something, they still show respect. I think they think that's the Church and its teachings, and they respect them.

Finally, one bishop shared some details of the disrespect he has experienced as a bishop:

Two years ago, [there was a case about] one of the teachers in one of our Catholic high schools. The pastor removed her and put her on leave because of her negativity. She was on Facebook against gay kids. I backed the pastor, and boy, did I get heat for it. A large segment of our church, those to the right of Attila the Hun, attacked me. I got 4,000 hate calls and e-mails in one week. They had put our phone number on [a conservative talk show], would you believe it? It was unbelievable, and these are exact quotes: "I'd like to talk to the f-ing bishop" or "the g-d bishop." And these calls were from so-called "upstanding" Roman Catholics. Well, you can have them. It was really horrendous. I thought my executive assistant was going to have a nervous breakdown.

It is fitting that we end this chapter on this controversial note of frustration because, as we describe in the next chapter, bishops are often involved in controversy and face many challenges every day.

4

Challenges, Hopes, Vocations

We need to engage in strategic thinking every day because we are in a culture that is changing so fast. A lot of bishops feel negatively about the post Vatican II world and feel the lack of attendance/participation is due to the changes made there. A lot of lay people feel that way too and that if we only get back to the Latin Mass the place will be packed. They think that the liturgy should focus not on community but on God, the transcendent. That is the fatal flaw—and that religious education was not taught properly and the catechesis wasn't proper.

The only problem with that theory is that the world has changed more since 1965 than it did in the 2,000 years before. I think of the computer, the cell phone, you name it. Are we going to be living on Mars? I think that we have not reacted to the future. I think many of us are still living in an ideal world that no longer exists and that we are not looking to the real future coming at us. Are we flexible enough to figure out what the message is going to mean there?

BISHOP FROM A DIOCESE IN THE EAST

THE PACE OF change in our modern world was dizzying in the 1960s and 1970s and has only accelerated in the current age of the Internet and instant communications. This chapter first looks at the challenges bishops face today, challenges that take on an entirely different importance in this time of instant communication. Second, we examine their hopes for the future. Where do the bishops find consolation and encouragement as they look to the future Church in the United States? Third, we look at how the bishops are encouraging vocations to priesthood and religious life. How are they promoting a new generation of priests, sisters, and brothers to serve the Church? These three issues provide a broad understanding of where the bishops of the United States may be leading the Church.

Challenges

As the leader of a diocese, the bishop confronts a seemingly endless stream of challenges: practical, financial, theological, and personal. Many of the challenges are common to any leadership position in or outside the Church, such as finances, personnel, real estate, and public relations. Others are more unique in terms of theology, faith, sacraments, and engagement with the civic culture in which the Church exists and functions.

In our survey of the bishops we asked them what they perceived to be the three greatest challenges to the Church in the United States today. As an open-ended question, the bishops were free to respond however they wished.

As Table 4.1 shows, 45 percent of the responding bishops wrote that secularism was one of three greatest challenges; 32 percent mentioned religious freedom, 15 percent said indifference or a loss of faith and practice, and 11 percent said moral relativism. The four challenges of secularism, religious freedom, indifference, and moral relativism arise from the larger social and civic environment of the United States in the early part of the 21st century.

About 15 percent of the bishops identified two other challenges: marriage and family life, and the need for more vocations to priesthood and

Table 4.1 Most Commonly Identified Challenges for the Church

"What do you perceive as the three greatest challenges to the Church in the U.S. today?"	%
Secularism	45
Religious freedom	32
Indifference, loss of faith, non-practicing	15
Marriage and family	15
Lack of priests, vocations	13
Relativism	11

Total does not add up to 100% because bishops named three issues.

Source: CARA Bishop Survey, 2016.

religious life. These two challenges are clearly influenced by the larger society but are also vocations within the Church to marriage, priesthood, and religious life. Fewer than 10 percent of the bishops identified any other challenges.

Secularism

The challenge of secularism is not an abstract or generic issue for the bishops but one that is clearly a part of their particular environment. When asked, practically all bishops, some 95 percent, agreed "somewhat" or "strongly" that "secular U.S. culture is hostile to the values of Catholicism." Additionally, 62 percent of the bishops said that "criticism in the secular press or media" was "somewhat" or "a great" problem to them on a day-to-day basis.

Religious Freedom

The issue of religious freedom has become more prominent in recent years with legislative and regulatory debates on gender identity, regulation of adoption services, same-sex marriage, vouchers for private schools, contraceptive access, and the provision of abortion services, among other issues. Dioceses and other Catholic organizations in the United States are the largest nongovernmental providers of education, health care, and social services in the nation. As such, legislative and regulatory issues impact the vast array of Catholic schools, hospitals, and social service centers serving tens if not hundreds of millions of Americans regardless of their personal religious affiliation. Numerous practical organizational policies and liabilities are at play in the realm of religious freedom for the bishops who are often the leaders, board members, and owners of these thousands of institutions.

A bishop from a southern diocese reflected:

I think in general, I would just call it an erosion of conscience rights and religious liberties and they did not begin with the Obama administration. They probably go back to the judicial philosophy of Oliver Wendell Holmes. They go back to legal positivism and so there has been a kind of a progressive limiting of the meaning of religious freedom. There has been a desire on the part of government to manage and regulate, not houses of worship so much, but the

works that we do that serve the common good, whether it's charities or schools. And there has been a limitation of conscience rights
there. The most famous, of course, is HHS mandate. There are also
licensure challenges, accreditation challenges, and local ordinances
that would take our teaching on marriage and sexuality and frame
it up as bigotry and discrimination and sort of put us in the box.
And then there is simply the encroaching secularization of the culture. The biggest challenge however with religious freedom as with
many other things is not legal or legislative, interesting as those
things are, it really is an evangelization challenge. Because the more
people who practice their faith, promote their faith and understand
its centrality in their life and that it's a whole way of life; the more
people who do that, they also vote differently and they take care of
the problem as it were. You know, I think winning hearts and minds
is the most difficult and the most basic thing that has to be done.

It is not a surprise that about one-third of the bishops perceive religious freedom as a great challenge to the Church in the United States
today. Nearly all of the bishops agreed "somewhat" or "strongly" that "the
Catholic Church's right to religious freedom faces increasing threat from
the government." Over 60 percent of the bishops say they have "often"
or "on a regular basis" written a pastoral letter or column in the diocesan
newspaper on the topic of religious freedom.

Indifference

During the past 20 years there has been a notable rise in the proportion of
Americans that identify their religious affiliation as "nothing in particular"
or "none." The percentage of nones was fairly small and stable for decades
and began increasing in the 1980s and 1990s. In 2016, these self-identified
"nones" were 21 percent of the population.[1] Even though the United States
is one of the most religiously engaged developed nations, the growth of the
"nones" is one indicator of an increasing religious indifference in the population. At the same time, there is a notable amount of religious churning
among practically all of the religious denominations—individuals leaving
the faith community they were raised in to join a different faith community,

1. Tom W. Smith, Peter Marsden, Michael Hout, and Jibum Kim, *General Social Surveys,
1972–2016* [Data file]. Chicago: NORC at the University of Chicago.

or no faith community, and some later returning to the faith community of their youth.[2] A bishop from a diocese in the Midwest said the greatest challenge is:

> the declining numbers in sacramental reception, declining numbers in attendance and this is a great cross, I know, for every bishop in the North. In the South they are building churches. They are still growing because of the influx of Hispanics particularly, but up here that can be a downer. That is a challenge. How do we re-evangelize?
>
> While some people leave because of an incident, something happened, somebody said something to them, [for] most people, it's just they fade away. It just happens. So there is not a lot of animosity out there in that great number of former [Catholics], we just have to somehow appeal to them to help them see the transcendental aspects of their life.

Indifference, a loss of faith, and the number of Catholics that do not practice their faith is identified as a major challenge for 15 percent of the bishops. Another one in ten bishops stated that moral relativism is a great challenge to the Church today. Indifference and relativism are two attitudes that can go hand in hand and reflect a perceived irrelevance for the Church or any faith community. A bishop from a diocese in the South said:

> I think secularization is becoming more and more dominant, as we know the most popular religion right now in the US is what they call the "nones", those who don't believe in anything. I think the sort of complexity, you know, that a lot of Catholics have about their relationship with Christ. I don't think we're going to hell in a handbasket, but I do think there is in general a lack of hunger for God or for truth. And as our society moves forward with same-sex marriage and a desire for women priests, these are all going to be complicated issues. And the whole issue with social media and technology, and how that plays into one's faith life . . .

2. Mark M. Gray, "Coming Home," *Nineteen Sixty-four*, April 22, 2011, http://nineteensixty-four.blogspot.com/2011/04/coming-home.html.

Relativism

A related difficulty is how to reach out and communicate with those who are no longer in the pews on Sunday, especially in a time of rapidly changing mediums of communication. More than four in five bishops said that the "difficulty of really reaching people today" is "somewhat" or "a great" problem.

The bishops identified two other major challenges, concerning the vocational choices of Catholics to marriage, priesthood, and religious life. About 15 percent of the bishops named these as a "great" challenge.

Marriage

The number of individuals in the United States entering into a Catholic marriage each year has declined from 1990, when there were 326,079 marriages, to 2016, with 145,916 marriages. At the same time, the Catholic population grew from 55,700,000 to 67,700,000.[3] There are 12,000,000 more Catholics but less than half as many marriages over the past 26 years. The decline in the number of marriages is a national phenomenon seen across the entire population, but the decline among Catholics is even greater. Pope Francis expressed his concern about marriage and family:

> The family is experiencing a profound cultural crisis, as are all communities and social bonds. In the case of the family, the weakening of these bonds is particularly serious because the family is the fundamental cell of society, where we learn to live with others despite our differences and to belong to one another; it is also the place where parents pass on the faith to their children.[4]

The structure of Catholic families has also changed. In a national poll of self-identified Catholic families with minor children living at home, 80 percent were married couples, 13 percent of families were a single parent living with a partner, and 5 percent were single, never-married parents. Approximately one in five Catholic children (21 percent) are growing up

---

3. *The Official Catholic Directory*, Vols. 1990 and 2016 (New Providence, NJ: P.J. Kenedy & Sons, 1990, 2016).

4. Pope Francis, *Apostolic Exhortation Evangelii Gaudium* (November 24, 2013), https://w2.vatican.va/content/francesco/en/apost_exhortations/documents/papa-francesco_esortazione-ap_20131124_evangelii-gaudium.html.

in a "nontraditional" family.[5] This current reality presents the local parish and diocese with many challenges for the pastoral care and inclusion of the family, the education of children, and the Church's understanding of marriage as a sacrament.

Priesthood/Religious Life

The response of Catholics to the vocational call to priesthood and religious life has also seen a dramatic decline in the number of individuals entering seminaries and novitiates. The steepest decline occurred in the 1970s and 1980s and continues today for religious life, though the number of diocesan priests being ordained has stabilized and even grown slightly in the past decade. Twenty years ago the ratio of Catholics per diocesan priest was 1,774 and in 2016 it had grown to 2,628.[6]

Fifty-six percent of bishops reported that "the image of the priesthood today" is "somewhat" or "a great" problem to them on a day-to-day basis. A similar proportion of bishops also said the "criticism from laity about priests" is a day-to-day problem. As the leader of the local diocesan Church, bishops are the ones responsible for personnel management and most especially for the diocesan priests. At the same time, bishops are confronted with the growing demand for more priests to minister to a growing and more culturally diverse Catholic population. Eighty-six percent of bishops reported that the "limited number of available priests" is a "somewhat" or "a great" administrative issue in their diocese.

Addressing Clergy Sexual Abuse and
Reaching Out to the Victims

A relatively small proportion of bishops—7 percent—explicitly mentioned the issue of the clergy sexual abuse crisis in response to the challenges question. As with several other issues, this percentage is small enough that it didn't make the threshold of 10 percent used as a cutoff for inclusion in Table 4.1. We hasten to add that some additional responses may refer to the abuse crisis less directly. Examples include "restoring trust/credibility"

---

5. CARA Catholic Poll [Data file]. Washington, DC: Center for Applied Research in the Apostolate, September 2015.

6. *The Official Catholic Directory*, Vols. 1996 and 2016.

and "hostile media." Even so, there were fewer references to the crisis than we expected. Given the obvious importance of the abuse problem for the Church, it is worth discussing here. In this short section we provide a brief view of how a few bishops feel about it. A full examination of the sexual abuse issue, and the bishops' response merits a book of its own.

We asked bishops about the topic in personal interviews. Below are two examples of how they described the challenge to the Church and to themselves in addressing the abuse problem (note that both were ordained to the episcopacy after the 2002 explosion in the media; the first speaker is an auxiliary bishop).

The USCCB took very specific steps at that time,[7] as did my diocese. By the time I became a bishop I did not feel the need to change anything, so I did not advocate for change [to policies] or anything like that. I really don't have much more to say about the policies that have been put into place. Here in [my diocese] our archbishop had addressed the situation quite well and handled a number of cases. What I have done is continue his pastoral outreach. We have a retreat center and we regularly have retreats for victims of sexual abuse. We have a separate retreat for victims of sexual abuse by a priest. That is about once a year. It is advertised and we usually get three, four, or five victims. I always sit in on a whole Saturday with them to hear their stories and basically to apologize in the name of the Church to them. Those are very painful experiences, and it made me even more angry at those priests who did these things.

My desk is a magnet for all the negativity in my diocese. There are many sizeable stacks of papers on my desk. One in particular has to do with the sexual abuse cases in my diocese, stretching back many years. It is all so sad. So much suffering! So much sadness! One frustrating aspect of all this is that most of these tragedies occurred before I was even ordained as a priest and, as you know, I did not grow up in this diocese, so it all happened before I ever lived here. And now it is my responsibility to deal with it, to somehow resolve it, to be accountable for it. A tall order indeed.

---

7. I.e., the *Charter* and *Essential Norms* adopted in the aftermath of the 2002 media coverage.

Fewer than half of current ordinaries became bishops prior to 2002. And only about one in five had been bishops for more than five years at that time. Of those, some were still auxiliary bishops with little involvement in decisions regarding sexual abuse cases. This is not to suggest that all those who were not ordinaries at the time were blameless or completely ignorant regarding the issue. Some had been involved in clergy personnel decisions while working in chancery positions (for example as a vicar general or vicar for clergy). But to get a perspective on 2002, we deliberately sought out a few interviewees who were already ordinaries at that time. These men faced the task of responding to the crisis forcefully, credibly, and with compassion and contrition toward the victims. One who had been an auxiliary for several years during the 1990s and then an ordinary for a short time spoke to us about the USCCB meeting in Dallas in June of 2002. At this meeting the U.S. Bishops developed common rules for all dioceses in handling clergy sexual abuse allegations (pending approval of the Pope John Paul II), codified in the *Charter for the Protection of Children and Young People*.[8] Within the Church, this document is colloquially referred to as the Dallas Charter. One of the most controversial provisions was the so-called "zero tolerance" rule. It dictated that any priest who had ever been credibly accused of abusing a minor, even once, must be immediately and permanently removed from ministry:

> My diocese always took abuse cases very seriously, and we did an investigation right away. I would say that in general, without realizing it, we were already following much of what the Dallas Charter ended up asking for. I did not see the need to modify anything my own dioceses did [when I became ordinary]. Of course, everything changed in 2002 because of the magnitude of the crisis, and because of the public dimension of the whole thing. I remember being in Dallas. It was absolutely the most tension-filled meeting I have ever been to. There were not just clouds over our heads but thunderstorms.
>
> The majority there agreed with the new proposals, but the thing that was a struggle for some bishops was the "one strike and you're out" approach. The question that kept coming up was: how do

---

8. United States Conference of Catholic Bishops, *Charter for the Protection of Children and Young People* (Washington, DC, 2018), http://www.usccb.org/issues-and-action/child-and-youth-protection/upload/Charter-for-the-Protection-of-Children-and-Young-People-2018. pdf.

justice and mercy come together? I think it became evident that because of the influence and power of the priest that even one strike was a betrayal of trust and so in the end, as we know, it was voted in. But I would say that some people really felt pain for those who had done something wrong once and had really repented and had truly found a new way of life. But the situation was such, and the betrayal of trust was such, that we felt that we had no other alternative.

This same bishop continued by discussing how he felt about the victims when the scandal broke and about his outreach to them:

I felt heartbroken because of the victims and because they had been so terribly hurt. I also felt heartbroken for the Church and its reputation, and the betrayal of trust—but my primary concern was for the victims and for what they have been through. In some cases, knowing some of the people abused, I certainly had compassion for them. I met with some of the victims [in 2002]. In all my years as a bishop, I have met with many, many victims. And every story is unique, but the common denominator is pain. Also, I have often found that they usually don't say anything for a long time and that silence makes their suffering all the more painful.

In contrast, some of our interviewees who were not yet bishops in 2002 had experiences similar to those of other, regular priests (see *Same Call, Different Men*[9] for an extensive discussion of the reaction of priests to the scandal). One whose ministry had been primarily in parishes and who was working at a seminary in 2002 described his reaction. He also discussed challenges raised by the scandal for the image of priesthood:

It took a while for me to fully understand the situation because it took a while for all the details to unfold, for the picture to fully emerge. For someone who was unaware of how serious this problem was, I admit that I found it confusing. At the very beginning the question that came to mind was: "How much of this is reality and how much is not?" . . . One would be hard-pressed to find a tougher or more damaging scandal in the history of the Church. I experienced

---

9. Mary L. Gautier, Paul M. Perl, and Stephen J. Fichter, *Same Call, Different Men: The Evolution of the Priesthood since Vatican II* (Collegeville, MN: Liturgical Press, 2012).

a tremendous sense of frustration and deep disappointment. Just thinking of the unimaginable victimhood of these innocent children was emotionally overwhelming. It was a very difficult time. . . .

Parish priests on the front lines were dealing with the outrage, the anger, and the frustration of so many good and devout Catholics. I had a different experience because I was at the seminary. I spoke with the seminarians about the issue. It would have been hard not to talk about it, as it was on the news all the time. The crisis did not shake their own confidence about the future, but it certainly affected their families' confidence about their sons' vocations. Their families had so many doubts about their future. They were shaken to the core. Remember that this was a time when priests were still held in such high esteem. For these families, the abuse scandal shattered the good image of the priesthood. Many of the parents were saying to their sons that they were wasting their time and energy becoming priests. . . . The image of the priesthood really went down the drain during the pedophilia crisis.

We used data from the survey to explore whether bishops' concerns about the image of the priesthood were related to media coverage of the scandal in their dioceses. As we noted earlier in this chapter, about six in ten bishops described the image of the priesthood as "somewhat" or "a great" problem. The survey also asked how much coverage the scandal had received in their current diocese, from "little or no coverage" to "extensive coverage." We found no significant relationship between these two variables. In other words, the extent to which bishops view the image of the priesthood as problematic is unrelated to intensity of coverage in their own diocese. We did, however, find a different relationship. Bishops were significantly more likely to say "the image of bishops today" is a problem for them if their diocese has experienced more intensive coverage of the scandal. Thus, bishops' perceptions of the public image of themselves, appears to be a more localized phenomenon. A section in Chapter 7 will address a somewhat related issue: the extent to which bishops said it was difficult for them to present or defend Church teaching because of coverage of the scandal in their dioceses.

For the book *Same Call, Different Men*,[10] Fichter and Perl conducted focus groups and personal interviews with priests. A common suspicion

---

10. Gautier et al., *Same Call, Different Men*.

voiced by priests at that time (2009–2011) was that the problem of abuse of minors and its cover-up was not limited to the Church. Many priests bristled at accusations from Church critics that something about Catholicism specifically (or religion generally) makes it uniquely susceptible to attracting and/or protecting predators. They were especially disdainful of the notion that a vow of celibacy can transform otherwise ordinary young men into pedophiles.[11] At that time, however, it was rather difficult for priests to point a finger at other specific organizations or institutions. By the time we conducted interviews for the present book, that was no longer the case. Scandals had erupted over abuse of minors under the purview of Penn State, USA Swimming, and USA Gymnastics/Michigan State. Reports of abuse and harassment in the entertainment industry (some involving minors) flooded the news media in 2017. Comments by bishops about these scandals did not strike us as triumphalist but rather as expressing hope that there can be a more fruitful reckoning with the problem of abuse in society if it is approached without the baggage of religious bias. One bishop said:

> I was presiding at a wedding on the west coast during the height of the scandal. I was talking privately with the father of the groom before the wedding began. This man was very bright and had spent years as a researcher [on the topic of pedophilia.] He said something to me that I thought was very curious at the time. He said it was a widespread illness and we were only dealing with a very small sample if we thought it only existed in the Catholic Church. He told me, "It's convenient for the rest of society, to place the blame for [pedophilia] on the Roman Catholic Church, but I can tell you as a researcher, this problem is not just in the Catholic Church but is actually widespread throughout many different sectors of society." Specifically, he said that it was in the field of entertainment as well and that there were just as many cover-ups as we've seen in the Church. He told me about a young actor who had been abused hundreds of times. How prophetic he was, especially in light of

---

11. As just one example, the HBO documentary *Celibacy*, released in 2004, explicitly posited a causal link between celibacy and child abuse. It was sharply criticized by the USCCB's Office of Film and Broadcasting. See Daniel Burke, "Catholic Bishops Denounce Film on Clerical Celibacy; Moviemaker Says HBO Documentary Aims to Go Beyond Headlines on Church Sex-Abuse Scandal," *Washington Post*, June 26, 2014, B7.

everything we've been reading about Harvey Weinstein,[12] and so many other people in Hollywood. It turns out, sadly, that he was very right. . . . Of course, there should be outrage when a priest is the one who commits the crime because he is supposed to represent Christ and uphold all the moral values that the Church tries to promote.

The greatest challenges to the Church in the United States identified by the bishops arise from the larger social and civic environment and from a shift in the number of individual Catholics discerning a call to sacramental marriage, priesthood, or religious life within the Church. So what are the hopes and dreams of the bishops through which these challenges will be addressed?

Hopes

As the leader of a local diocese, the bishop needs to focus a major portion of his time and energy on managing an organization with hundreds if not thousands of employees and a budget of tens or hundreds of millions of dollars. As the C.E.O. of an organization confronted with the identified challenges, what gives him hope for the future? What are the means to address these challenges? Are there organizational, personal, technical, theological, or communal resources to draw on?

We asked the bishops, "What three aspects of the Church in the United States today give you the greatest amount of hope?" As an open-ended question, the bishops were free to respond however they wished. We grouped their responses into eight major categories, shown in Table 4.2.

Half of the bishops named Catholic youth and young adults as their greatest hope, followed by the laity (30 percent) and vocations and seminarians (28 percent). About one-quarter of the bishops identified spirituality and sacraments, and priests as giving them the greatest hope. Sixteen

---

12. Nearly all Weinstein's public accusers were adults at the time of his alleged harassment and assaults. However, at least one, actress Kate Beckinsale, was 17 years old. Other prominent individuals in Hollywood, perhaps most notably actor Kevin Spacey, were accused in 2017 by multiple people who were underage at the time.

Christie D'Zurilla, "Kate Beckinsale: Harvey Weinstein 'Is an Emblem of a System that is Sick,'" October 12, 2017, http://www.latimes.com/entertainment/la-et-entertainment-news-updates-kate-beckinsale-harvey-1507827299-htmlstory.html.

Table 4.2 Most Commonly Identified Hopes for the Church

"What three aspects of the Church in the U.S. today give you the greatest amount of hope?"	%
Youth and young adults	51
Vocations and seminarians	28
Laity	27
Priests	24
Spirituality and sacraments	23
Pope Francis	16
Immigration, Hispanics, and diversity	15
Evangelization	15

Total does not add up to 100% because bishops named three issues.

Source: CARA Bishop Survey, 2016.

percent of the bishops named Pope Francis, and 15 percent of bishops listed immigration, Hispanics, and cultural diversity or evangelization.

Youth and Young Adults

That bishops identified Catholic youth and young adults as providing their greatest hope goes counter to the data that show a decline in marriages and baptisms, and participation in Catholic schools and parish religious education. The bishops' responses suggest that the young Catholics they meet and engage with are sources of encouragement and energy in the Church. The data on the participation of youth in the Church can be discouraging, yet the experience of those youth who are involved in the Church provides great hope to the bishops.

At the same time that many dioceses of the Northeast and Midwest have experienced a stable or diminishing Catholic population, dioceses in the South and West have had rapid growth. While there are proportionately more young Catholics in the South and West than in the Northeast and Midwest, there is no significant difference among the bishops of each region in naming youth and young adults as their greatest hope.

Laity

Twenty-seven percent of the bishops said the laity gave them the greatest amount of hope. It is notable that bishops in the Northeast (37 percent) are more likely than bishops in the Midwest (21 percent) and the West (23 percent) to express hope in the laity. This may be due to the sharp decline in the Northeast of number of priests and religious who traditionally provided so much of the pastoral ministry in the parishes. The role and participation of Catholic laity in the life of the Church has greatly changed in the decades following Vatican Council II. Dioceses and parishes now have active pastoral and finance councils where lay members have a voice in parish and diocesan decisions. Additionally, the increase of lay ecclesial ministers and employees in practically every work has created a local Church where lay women and men serve and have responsibility for nearly all dimensions of the Church's life.

"Conflict with parishioners or laity about issues of the day" is "very little" or "no" problem at all on a day-to-day basis for a majority of the bishops, though two in five bishops say that this is "somewhat" of a problem. At the same time, over half of the bishops say that "unrealistic demands and expectations of lay people" are "somewhat" of a problem on a day-to-day basis.

One source of these conflicts and tensions is the respect and attention that laity and priests give to one another in their respective roles in the local Church. There is a small but notable difference in how the bishops weigh this. While 87 percent of the bishops agreed that "Catholic laity are sufficiently respectful of the priest's authority," 76 percent agreed that "priests are sufficiently respectful of the voice of the laity." This suggests that the bishops perceive a slightly greater need for the priests to respect the voice of the laity than vice versa.

As the theological orientation of the bishop varies from traditional to moderate to progressive, so too does the likelihood of naming the laity as one of his sources for the greatest amount of hope. Only 15 percent of the self-identified traditional bishops named the laity as a source of great hope, compared to 35 percent of the moderate and 40 percent of the progressive bishops who did so. This suggests that the increasing prominence of lay leadership within the Church may be limited by the local bishop's theological orientation.

In a more particular area regarding the leadership of women in the local Church, 87 percent of the bishops agreed that "women should have more leadership roles in parishes," and 78 percent agreed that "women should have more leadership roles in my diocese." The great majority of bishops see an increasing leadership role for lay women in the local Church. The chancellor is the highest "ecclesial" or decision-making office a layperson can hold in the Church and is often ranked second or third in authority after the bishop in a diocese. In 2016, 31 percent of the diocesan chancellors were lay or religious women and 42 percent were priests.[13] Women chancellors are as common among the largest dioceses as they are among the smallest.

Spirituality and Sacraments

About one-quarter of the bishops named spirituality and the sacraments as giving them the greatest amount of hope. This is evident as practically all the bishops reported that the "joy of administering the sacraments and presiding over the liturgy" is an important source of satisfaction. A similar proportion of bishops also said that "being part of a community of Christians who are working together to share the Good News of the Gospel" and "preaching the Word" are important sources of satisfaction. The personal experience of bishops as pastors and sacramental ministers grounds their hope in the efficacy of sacraments and spirituality to sustain and build up the Church.

When asked in an interview what particular role he found most rewarding or consoling, a bishop in the Midwest responded:

> I would probably say to sanctify, I love confirmands and I just love doing Confirmations. . . . or celebrating a big Mass like Christmas Mass or ordinations. Gathering the people together and leading worship with them, I find that very, very enjoyable. I tend to be kind of a people person, so I like to be with people.

Vocations and Seminarians

Over one-quarter of the survey respondents identified seminarians and vocations to priesthood and religious life as giving them the greatest hope. This response is notably less than the hope they find in young adults in the Church.

---

13. Mary L. Gautier, "Did You Know? Female Chancellors," *Nineteen Sixty-four*, August 25, 2016, http://nineteensixty-four.blogspot.com/2016/08/did-you-know-female-chancellors.html.

Pope Francis and Priests

Pope Francis and the priests of their diocese are among the greatest hopes for a number of the bishops. This hope, though, is not blind to the challenges of authority, divisions, and criticism. Three in ten bishops say that "the way authority is exercised in the Church" is a problem on a day-to-day basis, and four in ten say that "theological divisions among my priests" is a problem. Over half of the bishops acknowledged that "criticism from laity about priests" is a day-to-day problem.

Immigration

Between 1980 and 2015, there were a sizable number of immigrants coming to the United States, many of them Catholic. In 1980, approximately 10 percent of the adult Catholics were foreign-born and over the past thirty-five years that has increased to 27 percent of the adult Catholic population.[14] This scale of Catholic immigrants coming to the United States has not been seen in a hundred years, and at that time (1890–1920) the Church dealt with many conflicts, divisions, and even schism in its efforts to incorporate a primarily European immigration stream. In recent years, the European Catholic immigrants are fewer in number, compared to the Latin American, Asian, and African immigrant populations. The cultural and ethnic diversity of recent Catholic immigrants is more distinctive than in the past.

A bishop from the West, where the Catholic population is growing and becoming more diverse reflected:

> In a certain sense, the immigrant Catholicism from Mexico, I think, is probably a little more robust than what we have from the European immigrants. Not much, the Hispanic families don't "get their shorts in a bunch" if a son or daughter comes out as gay, they "don't get their shorts in a bunch" if one of their daughters gets pregnant, they kind of go with it. They don't quite understand it, they don't quite get it, but everybody has a place at the table and you just kind of work with it. You uphold the values and you make sure the family is together. Whether you have somebody who is dealing drugs or

---

14. Smith et al. 2015, General Social Survey, relevant years; U.S. Census Bureau, International Data Base, relevant years.

somebody else is a priest, you know there is a kind of resiliency that I don't think was as present in the European immigrant families and certainly the brittleness in North American culture around politics and sociology that has really created great fragility on the faith of the English side. So the Spanish side feels a lot more robust and able to kind of deal with [problems]. Mexican families are in a variety of places and they kind of hold together because there is a certain resilience and even a muscular flexibility to deal with folks struggling with temptations and weaknesses in a variety of ways. The English side can be a little bit more tribal. That is kind of what affects the faith because people touch faith sometimes through a wedding sometimes through a family tragedy, sometimes by just hanging out, and I mean they are able to be Catholic in a variety of ways in Spanish. I wonder about that kind of religious cultural glue long term and how do you pass on the faith?

One in seven bishops said that immigration, Hispanics, and cultural diversity gives them the greatest amount of hope. The bishops experience the growing cultural and ethnic diversity of the Church in the United States as a source of hope rather than as a challenge for the Church.

Evangelization

Finally, the bishops named efforts at evangelization as one of their greatest hopes. Practically all of the bishops said that "being part of a community of Christians who are working together to share the Good News of the Gospel" is an important satisfaction in their life and work as a bishop.

It is interesting to contrast the challenges and hopes of the bishops. The greatest challenges are external forces of the dominant culture that conflict with the community of faith (Catholic or otherwise): secularism, indifference, and restrictions on religious freedom. In contrast, the greatest hopes are internal: the youth and the laity of the Church, as well as the Catholic faithful.

The secondary level of perceived challenges are marriage, family life, and vocations to the priesthood and religious life. These are internal features of the Church's life and health that have been diminishing over the past several decades in the United States. The secondary level of hopes are spirituality, sacraments, vocations, and seminarians, each of which sustains and strengthens the features being challenged.

In sum, what we heard from the bishops is that the external cultural and social forces that threaten the life of the Church can be addressed by the youth and laity of the Church through spirituality and sacraments.

Vocations to Priesthood

When asked to identify the greatest challenge for the Church, many bishops named the lack of priests and vocations (13 percent). At the same time, when asked to identify their greatest hope, 28 percent named vocations and seminarians. Vocations to priesthood are *both* a great challenge and a great hope. How do the bishops experience this tension between challenge and hope?

All of the bishops of the United States are confronted with the need to find a sufficient number of priests to lead the parishes in their diocese. Nearly nine in ten bishops said that the "limited number of available priests" is a day-to-day problem in administering their diocese. The strategy that practically every bishop states he has or will use to address this need is to increase local vocation efforts. Yet this strategy itself has its challenges. More than half the bishops reported that "the image of the priesthood today" is "somewhat" or "a great" problem for them on a day-to-day basis. The image of the priest in the public imagination is not necessarily positive or inviting to younger men who are discerning their vocational call in life.[15]

Compounding the public image of priests is the experience of about one-half of the bishops that the "theological divisions among my priests" is an ongoing problem, as is the "criticism from the laity about priests." It should come as no surprise, then, when about one-half of the bishops said that priest morale is a daily problem for them. But the bishops' perception does not mean that the individual priest is unhappy or unsatisfied in his vocation and ministry. In a national survey of diocesan priests, Rossetti and Rhoades concluded:

> Contrary to popular myths, Catholic priests appear to be very satisfied in their callings, with their satisfaction rates among the highest in the country. Moreover, priests appear to feel good about

---

15. Jim Norman, "Americans Rate Healthcare Providers High on Honesty, Ethics," *Gallup*, December 19, 2016, http://www.gallup.com/poll/200057/americans-rate-healthcare-providers-high-honesty-ethics.aspx.

themselves and profess to have a strong relationship to God and close friends. They report having a strong network of personal and spiritual supports, which likely act as a bulwark against burnout, despite their demanding work schedules.[16]

Over one-quarter of the bishops identified vocations and seminarians as one of their greatest hopes and one-fifth specifically mentioned the priests of their diocese. So while the bishop may be grappling with innumerable priest personnel issues and tensions, they also find hope in their seminarians and in many of the priests serving in their diocese. This is aptly expressed by a bishop in the West:

> I would be nothing as a bishop without my priests—nothing. This is especially the case since so many of the younger and active clergy are Hispanic. Most of the younger clergy speak Spanish as a first language, as do most of our parishioners. This is why my priests are everything to me as a bishop. We are close. They light the way for me. I would not be able to travel spiritually as a bishop without them. That is not to say that we are tension-free. We're not.

Individual bishops emphasized different vocation strategies, and personally involve themselves in encouraging young men in their discernment. One bishop from a diocese in the South participates in small group meetings with high school aged men and their parents:

> People, good Catholics, open their homes. I will go there on a Saturday and there might be fourteen, fifteen young people there in somebody's house and it's a very supportive atmosphere and we talk about the possibility of vocations with them. We engage, we have lunch we ask them questions. Then I meet with their parents afterwards and it doesn't take all that long. But I think it's done a lot to build vocations and awareness. I am beginning to build up campus ministry at [local universities] and already we are seeing some vocations from there. I think it's hugely important.

---

16. Stephen J. Rossetti and Colin J. Rhoades, "Burnout in Catholic Clergy: A Predictive Model Using Psychological and Spiritual Variables," *Psychology of Religion and Spirituality* 5, no. 4 (2013): 335–341.

The same occurs with seminarians studying for the diocese, where the bishop is concerned with the seminarian's practical preparation to minister to the People of God in that particular diocese. A bishop from an agricultural diocese has his seminarians spend a summer joining the field workers on the farms so that they can share in the hard work and struggles of the families they will care for as a pastor in years to come:

> My thought is this: if you want to elevate the bread and the wine, the gift to the earth and the work of human hands, and want to be worthy to do that, you should know the work that went into the bread and the wine. Because when we offer Eucharist, we are offering not simply the bread and wine, we are asking God to transform all of these gifts of human labor. So I really want the seminarians to know the labor that goes into it. And know the lives of the people that provide what we have, which really constitutes a huge part of the diocese. It's also that they begin to know the human side. Honestly, the general pastoral challenge is that . . . people tend to formulate moral values from the world of politics but they identify more with their politics than with their religion. Whether it's left or right. So you know the work experience in the field depoliticizes the seminarians and re-evangelizes them to look at life through the lens of the faith rather than the political lens, which is kind of the default position.

As the leader of a diocese, bishops are acutely aware of the problems, challenges, and frailties of their priests. The bishop is also aware of the excitement, zeal, and generosity of the seminarians and those still discerning a calling to priesthood.

Managing the priests, deacons, religious and lay personnel that minister to the people of the diocese is examined in the next chapter. A key element of that management is the bishop's own style and choice of collaboration.

5

Personnel and Collaboration

*The priests, I have to say, have been really, really good.
They have been patient, they have been supportive. I think
they have responded pretty well. Now having said that,
no one has 100 percent approval rating. Some people like
what you do and some people don't. Some of the priests will
be your faithful followers and supporters and other priests
don't like what you are doing at all. That is part of the
human experience and you have to be somewhat comfort-
able with that, but for the most part I would say the priests
have been terrific.*

BISHOP FROM A NORTHEASTERN DIOCESE

*I tried to put a decent team in and I wanted a team that
represented the Church, so I wanted staff that were clergy,
religious, and lay, to convey not only to the people but to
the priests, that this is Church: laity, religious, and clergy.*

. . .

*I realized when I became a bishop that I did not have all
the answers. I am not God. I needed to get input, collaboration, and insight, and I can't get it all by myself. You
have to get it from the outside and from people who have
the expertise to help make that decision.*

A RETIRED BISHOP

THIS CHAPTER CONSIDERS the bishop's role as leader of an organization whose primary resources are people. The first section explores the
bishops' perspectives and experiences with different types of church personnel. The second section discusses how bishops rely on different individuals and groups to assist in their decision-making. The final section

looks beyond the diocese to relationships with fellow bishops, both individually and as part of national and state bishops' conferences.

Relationships with Church Personnel

Bishops rely on priests, deacons, religious brothers and sisters, and lay people to serve in ministries within the Church. The bishops' relationships and interactions with different types of church personnel vary depending on the canonical status of the person. Two documents from Vatican II categorize people differently. *Lumen Gentium* identified three categories: (1) bishops, priests, and deacons are all ordained clergy and members of the hierarchy; (2) religious brothers and sisters are not ordained but have a special status because of their consecration through religious vows; (3) lay people are not ordained and are not members of religious orders.[1] *Perfectae Caritatis* defined two categories, ordained and lay. By this definition, religious brothers and sisters are also lay people because they are not ordained.[2]

Although both priests and deacons are ordained and accountable to the bishop as a religious superior, they have different employment statuses. Priests are generally full-time personnel. After the permanent diaconate was reinstated following Vatican II, deacons typically served in part-time, voluntary capacities. More recently, some deacons are serving as full-time church employees. In *Co-Workers in the Vineyard of the Lord*, the bishops discussed the role of lay ecclesial ministers, highlighting their status as full-time church personnel in contrast to the laity in general.[3] As in *Lumen Gentium, Co-Workers* distinguished lay persons from members of religious orders even though both are non-ordained. Religious engage in church ministry because of their consecration to religious life.

The next several sections of this chapter explore each of the different personnel types. Priests receive extended coverage because they are the bishops' primary collaborators.

---

1. Second Vatican Council, *The Dogmatic Constitution on the Church: Lumen Gentium*, November 21, 1964, http://www.vatican.va/archive/hist_councils/ii_vatican_council/documents/vat-ii_const_19641121_lumen-gentium_en.html.

2. Second Vatican Council, *Decree on the Up-to-Date Renewal of Religious Life: Perfectae Caritatis*, October 28, 1965, http://www.vatican.va/archive/hist_councils/ii_vatican_council/documents/vat-ii_decree_19651028_perfectae-caritatis_en.html.

3. United States Conference of Catholic Bishops, *Co-Workers in the Vineyard of the Lord* (Washington, DC, 2005), http://www.usccb.org/laity/laymin/co-workers.pdf.

Priests

A bishop has a different employment relationship with diocesan priests than with religious or extern priests,[4] deacons, religious brothers and sisters, or lay people. A bishop can terminate a diocesan priest from a church position, but he is responsible for priests in a different way than other personnel. If a deacon, religious, or lay person leaves a diocesan position the bishop is not responsible for their subsequent job placement as he is for diocesan priests.

The survey results give evidence of a complex relationship between bishops and priests. All but one of 127 responding bishops agreed that he felt accepted by the priests in his current diocese and 72 percent agreed "strongly." Consistent with this, 79 percent of bishops had "very little" or "no" problem with criticism from priests. However, 75 percent of bishops reported that priest personnel issues were "somewhat" or "a great" problem. Priest personnel issues can manifest in several forms, such as a specific problem with a particular priest, greater complexity in dealing with a problem because it involves a priest, or the problem of a limited number of available priests needed to fill the required positions.

Feeling accepted perhaps reflects the brother–priest role, and experiencing criticism or personnel problems are more related to the employer role. While these could be distinct experiences for the bishop, there is a strong relationship among the three measures. Bishops who experience priest personnel issues and criticism from priests as more problematic are more likely to agree only "somewhat," and not "strongly," that they feel welcomed and accepted by the priests.

In the survey from *Same Call Different Men,* 65 percent of priests reported their relationship with the bishop was "no" problem or "very little" problem.[5] Although the questions are different, we can take the bishop measures of "acceptance" and "lack of criticism" from priests as roughly comparable to the priest measure of having "no" problem with the bishop. However, each priest is responding in reference to one bishop, while each bishop is responding about a group of priests. Noting the limitation in comparing the two surveys, about two-thirds of priests

---

4. Extern priests are diocesan priests ordained in (and for) one diocese but temporarily serving in another diocese.

5. Mary L. Gautier, Paul M. Perl, and Stephen J. Fichter, *Same Call, Different Men: The Evolution of the Priesthood since Vatican II* (Collegeville, MN: Liturgical Press, 2012).

reported relatively good relationships with their bishops compared to about three-quarters of bishops reporting relatively good relationships with their priests.

The interviews provided an opportunity for bishops to elaborate on their relationships with priests. A prior auxiliary bishop and relatively new ordinary described the multifaceted nature of the relationship:

> I've always stressed with the priests the documents on the role of the bishop with his priests, it says they're collaborators with me. And I've told them countless times, I can't do anything without the priests. I can't do it. I'm supposed to be a brother, a priest and a friend to them. That's a hard thing to do. How are you a brother, a priest, and a friend to them when some of these guys are older than you? But it's working out.

Another bishop highlighted the challenge of the bishop–priest relationship and how the leader role impacts the brother-priest role:

> I do find it's very difficult to have friends in your own diocese. Because from an ecclesial point of view, you are everyone's supervisor so you might think you have a priest friend and all of a sudden you have to make a decision that does not sit well, and all of a sudden that friend is not quite as friendly as he used to be. Or, you have to make difficult decisions about transferring priests or disciplining priests or closing parishes or closing the schools. I find it very difficult to have close friends in my own diocese. That is not to say that people are not friendly and it's not to say that they don't care or are not supportive, but in terms of having close personal lifelong friends, I have not found that easy to do in my own diocese.

A bishop who grew up in the diocese which he now leads shared a similar reflection, highlighting the tension between being "brother-priest" and being "bishop:"

> Sometimes it is difficult to take on the role of bishop because there are times when they [priests] see me not as a bishop, but either as a teacher or a friend or someone they socialize with. I must say that one of my fears was in working with the priests, because I taught most of them in the seminary, or they were older than I, but that

has proven to be an unfounded fear. The priests have been most welcoming and most cooperative.

The survey results support the bishops' statements about the challenges of developing or maintaining friendships with priests in the diocese. Only 8 percent agreed "strongly" that most of their closest priest friends are in their current diocese. An additional 21 percent "somewhat" agreed with this statement. Bishops who grew up in the diocese where they currently serve (11 out of the 127 respondents) were more likely to agree that their closest priest friends are in the diocese. Bishops who have been in the diocese longer (as bishop) were more likely to agree "somewhat" or "strongly" that their closest friends are in the diocese. The bishops quoted earlier mentioned some difficulty in being friends with priests who were older than they are. The survey responses confirm that this is a more general experience. The older the bishop, the more likely he was to agree that his closest priest friends are in the diocese. Bishops with longer tenure were also more likely to report having friends in the diocese, and there is a positive correlation between age and tenure. When both factors are considered together, tenure remains significant while age does not.

The interviews give evidence that the bishops actively work to develop their relationships with priests. A recently appointed ordinary focused on the simple yet personal efforts he makes to relate to his priests:

> I think that the priests are so touched when I call them for something that maybe it's a birthday or an anniversary, or most recently I heard that one of the priests fell, one of the older priests. When you call them, it's "oh my gosh, thanks for calling." They appreciate the smallest thing. It's hard to be a friend and a brother and a bishop to people who might be older or younger, or your peers. How do you fulfill all that? And part of that is I just have to let them know that I care.

This bishop also described more structured ways of relating with his priests as well as fostering the priests' relationships with each other:

> The challenge I think in our diocese would be because guys are so spread out. There can be that tendency to do the lone ranger type thing. That's why it's important that once a month we have a day of recollection. It's a simple schedule, but part of it is just for

comradery. . . . Because our guys don't have the chance to see each other too often. I would say that's a big challenge, trying to foster the comradery of the priests.

Bishops' schedules make it difficult to foster relationships with priests. In the survey, 83 percent of bishops reported wanting to spend more time with the priests, and 60 percent said they felt too busy to be available to counsel all the priests.

In an interview, one bishop suggested spending time together is a mutual desire for priests and bishops:

I hear through channels that the younger pastors would like more kind of open support from me. I don't mean open, like, talking about them in public, but maybe getting together with them more often or being more just a little more intentionally encouraging of them. So I think I could probably do better at that. I think probably as simple as lunches with little groups of them or dinners, something like that. I'm actually in the process of trying to schedule some of those. I don't think it's real complicated, but I think it's that they are looking for a little more attention from me, in a healthy way.

This response described a form of relating that is somewhere between "spending time" and "counseling," further emphasizing the multilayered bishop–priest relationship.

One bishop described his early experience and initial difficulties with priests:

I walked into a very negative situation. There was a lot of factionism, a lot of in-fighting. You had clergy not talking to clergy, stuff like that. I was not afraid to bring in a priest to discuss a problem we were having with him. They weren't used to that. There was a certain amount of alienation because you had to put your foot down, because for almost seven years there was almost no direction. At times I got cooperation and at times I didn't. And again, it was from the faction. We had a certain group that never came to anything. Then you have your loners. Then you got your groupies who do whatever they want. It was a very fractured presbyterate [members of the priesthood] that I inherited.

A bishop from the West recounted a similar early experience that improved over time:

> When I first arrived here I have to say there was a lot of negativity. You could almost see the venom. But over the course of time, thanks be to God, a lot of that has dissipated. I feel very grateful to God that we have finally turned the middle ground of the presbyterate. There are still a few older cranky priests out there who still create some negativity but it's a lot different from when I first started here.

Although it might be reasonable to expect bishops to feel more accepted as time goes by, the survey results indicate no influence of tenure in the diocese on the difference between bishops agreeing "somewhat" versus "strongly" that they felt accepted by the priests.

For bishops who grew up in the diocese they now lead, becoming "the bishop" involves a transition in their role and a change in their relationship with fellow priests. One bishop reflected:

> In my home diocese, I came from that presbyterate. Of course I had been in chancery work and that kind of puts you in a relationship of what you were presumed to have authority over your fellow priest at one level or another. I always tried to downplay that as much as I could, but it was sort of inevitable because I had to be involved in very difficult situations. That certainly complicates your relationships with your priests. Amazingly, to this day, I have, I think very good relationships with many of the priests that I came up with, including my classmates, and many warm feelings about my home diocese.

Whether or not a bishop is leading the diocese he grew up in can affect his initial experience as bishop as well as the relationship with the priests of the diocese.

One bishop described the advantages of coming from outside the diocese:

> I think one of the advantages is that the priests serving in that diocese are of the opinion that with regard to them personally, you come in with a clean slate about them, so there are no preconceived notions. I think it's probably a good thing for the priests that you

don't know them. I think the second advantage is that you come in with an objective opinion about the diocese and maybe about some of the challenges and troubles that the diocese faces. You can be very objective about that. I think sometimes an expert is someone who lives two hours away. People are more receptive when you are coming in from the outside. There is a notion that bishops come from elsewhere.

The same bishop described the disadvantages:

The reverse of everything I just said. You don't know the priests. You come in and don't know them and so you have to rely on the vicar general to let you know who they are. You don't know the diocese. You can't hit the ground running. Just as there is welcome for outsiders, there is a distrust of outsiders. It's hard to come from somewhere else—another diocese.

The survey included a variety of questions asking bishops to consider some of the challenges they face. Table 5.1 shows survey responses specifically related to priest issues. Some of these concerns are shared by priests, so the table also shows the priests' responses to the same questions from *Same Call, Different Men.*[6]

Table 5.1 Source of Problems

"How much of a problem are each of the following to you on a day-to-day basis?"	"Somewhat" or a "Great" Problem	
	Bishops (%)	Priests (%)
Limited available priests	86	66
Working with international priests	64	31
Criticism from laity about priests	57	
Priest morale	47	
Theological differences among priests	41	43[a]
Criticism from priests	21	

[a] The *Same Call, Different Men* question is about theological differences in the concept of the priesthood

Sources: CARA Bishop Survey, 2016; Gautier et al., 2012.

6. Gautier et al., *Same Call, Different Men.*

Both bishops and priests experience the limited number of available priests as a notable problem, but bishops reported this at a higher rate than priests (86 versus 66 percent). This is understandable, because a primary impact of not enough priests is the difficulty in staffing parish leadership positions. The bishop would always be affected by this situation, but not all of the priests would be directly affected.

Bishops reported working with international priests as "somewhat" or "a great" problem at over twice the rate as priests. Bishops potentially have more interactions with international priests, so they are also more likely to have more negative interactions. In addition, the supervisory nature of the bishop–priest relationship and the issues bishops need to deal with related to international priests could make the same situation with an international priest more problematic for the bishop than it is for a local priest who might be involved.

A bishop from a Midwest diocese succinctly identified two common concerns regarding international priests, language and culture:

> We also have some diocesan Indian priests serving in the diocese. These are really holy, holy guys, but language problems are there and they will admit that is the case, and there are some cultural issues. They are not as assertive and as outgoing as our guys. They come across as really holy, good people. People generally admire that. The frustrating thing is the language at times.

The United States Conference of Catholic Bishops (USCCB) encourages all international ministers coming to the United States to participate in an orientation program and receive ongoing support through peer groups and mentoring. The bishops also recognize the need for cultural orientation for the receiving parish.[7] One approach some bishops have taken to address cross-cultural issues is to have men from other countries who are planning on becoming priests in U.S. dioceses attend seminary and prepare for the priesthood in the United States.[8]

---

7. United States Conference of Catholic Bishops, *Guidelines for Receiving Pastoral Ministers in the United States.* Third Edition (Washington, DC, 2014).

8. Mary L. Gautier, Melissa A. Cidade, Paul M. Perl, and Mark M. Gray, *Bridging the Gap: The Opportunities and Challenges of International Priests Ministering in the United States* (Huntington, IN: Our Sunday Visitor Inc., 2014).

Issues related to international priests might be more out of concern for them, rather than a problem per se. A bishop from a Midwestern diocese described efforts by the priests' council to address the needs of international priests:

> We've been looking at the question of international priests that serve with us here, that's one thing. I think we've gotten some good aspects about those challenges on the table. I don't know if we've solved any-thing exactly, but I think as a result we have more intentional repre-sentation from that group on our priests' council and have had a sort of working group to see what the particular challenges those men face and how we might be more understanding and respectful of that, as a group.

The survey results show an interesting relationship between how much of a problem bishops reported with international priests and how supportive or not they were of bringing more. While 64 percent of bishops reported that working with international priests was at least "somewhat" of a problem, 56 percent were also at least "somewhat" supportive about bringing more international priests. In other words, one-third of the bishops who had "some" problem with international priests also expressed "some support" for having more of them. One explanation could be that these bishops also have a problem with the limited number of available priests, so they might need more international priests. However, the survey results do not sup-port this conclusion. There is not a three-way relationship between these three measures. It could be that these bishops find the benefits outweigh the challenges.

Almost half of the bishops (48 percent) identified "criticism from laity about priests" as being "somewhat" of a problem. An additional 9 percent described it as "a great" problem. Almost half (47 percent) of bishops also re-ported that priest morale was "somewhat" or "a great" problem. When asked about criticism from priests (about the bishop), 21 percent responded that it was "somewhat" or "a great" problem. Bishops who found criticism from priests to be more of a problem were also more likely think that priest morale was a problem.

The bishop survey included a question asking about their experience with the theological differences among priests. The question for priests in the *Same Call, Different Men* survey was more specifically about theological

differences [among priests] in the concept of priesthood.⁹ If priests' views
on the concept of priesthood are consistent with their other theological
perspectives, then it is reasonable to compare the different questions for
bishops and priests. About 40 percent of both bishops and priests reported
that theological differences among priests was "somewhat" or "a great"
problem.

A bishop who is getting close to retirement expressed some concern about the kind of young men who are presenting themselves at
seminaries today:

> I think the challenge is, what is the model of priest we are looking
> for? If this view, the *ad orientem* view [a traditionalist approach which
> has the priest facing the altar and not the congregation] is going to
> be the view then you are only going to have a certain amount of
> priests you will be attracting. Are you only going to attract priests
> who are narcissists, who have an innate feeling of superiority or
> feelings of inadequacies? What are the interpersonal skill levels you
> will be attracting? I see a high percentage of those actively involved
> in church activities as being pretty narcissistic and that is a very
> dangerous path. . . . We have to be careful that we choose priests
> who are emotionally mature.

When considering all of the specific priest problems together, priest
morale, criticism from priests, and the limited number of available
priests had the greatest effect on the likelihood of bishops reporting
that "priest personnel issues" were "somewhat" or "a great" problem.
Also taking into account relevant bishop and diocesan characteristics,
the only significant factor is theological orientation. Bishops who identified as having a moderate theological perspective were less likely than
traditional or progressive bishops to report priest personnel issues as
being "somewhat" or "a great" problem. It is difficult to speculate as to
why this might be the case, but perhaps being "in the middle" allows
moderate bishops to accommodate priests on either side of the theological spectrum.

---

9. Gautier et al., *Same Call, Different Men.*

Non-Priest Personnel

In contrast to the 75 percent of bishops expressing concern about priest personnel issues, only 39 percent of bishops identified non-priest personnel issues as "somewhat" or "a great" problem. This may not be because bishops experience more personnel issues with priests compared to non-priests. It could be that nature of the bishop priest relationship makes priest personnel issues more complicated or problematic than non-priest personnel issues. The same type of personnel issue might need to be handled differently for priests than for non-priests.

Deacons

Deacons promise obedience to the diocesan bishop as an ecclesial superior. However, unlike priests, deacons are not typically available as full-time staff. Deacons usually have other full-time jobs and serve the church in a voluntary capacity. They are often attached to a parish and assist with Sunday liturgy. They are able to preside at weddings, baptisms and funerals, which helps with the sacramental workload of priests. Deacons have also traditionally engaged in charitable works, such as prison ministry. When deacons do serve in full-time ministerial roles such as parish ministers and chancery staff, their employment status is similar to that of a lay person rather than a priest.

In 2015, the number of permanent deacons (17,896) exceeded the number of active diocesan priests (15,751).[10] All but one diocese had at least one deacon, and all but eight had at least ten. In some dioceses deacon formation is done in cohorts so ordinations are every two or four years, depending on the length of the formation program. In a recent four-year period, between 2012 and 2015, at least one permanent deacon was ordained in 142 of the 177 dioceses, indicating that at least 80 percent of dioceses have an active diaconate program.

When asked about their relationships with deacons, bishops responded with a variety of perspectives. A bishop from a midwestern diocese described a very positive relationship:

> We have a great group of permanent deacons. I love them dearly.
> I know some bishops really do not care for permanent diaconate,
> I really value it a great deal. . . . They are really good and I think

---

10. *The Official Catholic Directory*, Vol. 2016 (New Providence, NJ: P.J. Kenedy & Sons, 2016).

priests by and large make great use of them. They are a happy group too.

A bishop with a large number of deacons recognized the need for additional deacons to represent specific ethnic communities within the diocese:

> I have a couple hundred. This is one of the first dioceses that re-instituted the diaconate after it was possible in the 70s. . . . We use them in a lot of ways. They are a variety of ages, of course, by now. We have a real good formation program and I ordain a group every other year. One of the challenges right now is to try to find—assuming the Lord is calling them—good candidates in the Hispanic community.

A reflection from a bishop from the South highlights his clear distinction between priests and deacons:

> That [relationship with deacons] is a little bit more difficult. I would say it's okay. Only because I don't allow them to wear clerics. I call them to ministry outside of just liturgical ministry on a weekend. I'm very much aware that the role of the deacon is to assist in those places where it is very difficult for the priest to be present. That's what I try to do with the permanent deacons and they're not always open to that because they want to be in their home parish on Sunday at one Mass a weekend. And that's not what it means to be a permanent deacon. . . . The struggle is lots of times they want to be clerics which makes them equal to a priest but they don't want to be held to that type of accountability or responsibility. They want to be deacons when it is convenient for them and to leave them alone when it's not.

Although *Lumen Gentium*[11] is clear that deacons—by their ordination—are clerics, for this bishop the distinguishing status is priesthood, not ordination. A bishop from the West made a similar distinction and described

---

11. Second Vatican Council, *Lumen Gentium*.

deacons more as higher status laity rather than lower status clergy, and expressed a generally more critical view:

> I must admit that I don't really have a close relationship with them. To be honest, I don't really have a high regard for the majority of them. Those who are involved in prison ministry are truly excellent but so many of those in parishes are not well-prepared. I call it the "monsignorization of the laity." We're trying hard to improve the training of the present class of deacons in formation and I recognize that overall my relationship with them needs improvement. That's something on me. Those previous generations of permanent deacons really didn't receive good training. They never had to take a single exam in preparation for the diaconate.

This bishop is responding to his concern by working to improve the deacon formation program. He also recognized his need to work on having a relationship with his deacons. Despite his concerns he seems to be planning on continuing the diaconate program.

The number of deacons is on the rise, as is the presence of deacons in full-time Church ministries. In contrast, the number of religious brothers and sisters is declining. Deacons, as well as lay people, are filling some of the vacancies left by retiring religious.

Religious Brothers and Sisters

Working with women and men's religious orders ranked low on the list of problem areas for bishops. One-fifth (20 percent) of the bishops indicated that working with women's religious orders was "somewhat" or "a great" problem and 18 percent reported "some" problem with men's religious orders. It is difficult to determine the nature of the problems based just on the survey questions. It could be about religious orders causing problems of some kind, or it could be related to the aging and diminishment of orders and the bishop needing to be involved in some way.

For both men and women religious, when considering multiple bishop and diocesan characteristics, including theological orientation, the only significant factor was the size of the diocese. Bishops from more populous dioceses were more likely to report higher levels of problems. This could be because larger dioceses are more likely to have larger numbers of individual religious brothers and sisters as well as greater diversity in religious orders.

The survey focused on bishops' experiences with religious orders. The interviews asked bishops about relationships with religious sisters. The interview responses included comments related to the religious orders and their institutional presence, as well as individual sisters. A bishop from the South expressed appreciation for the diversity of religious orders in his diocese:

> I get along very well with them. Some of the things they are doing may not be my cup of tea, but the arms of the Church are wide. If you are doing something that the Church allows you to do, I'm all in. So if your thing is social justice, that's fine with me. Go right ahead. I'm glad. I'm delighted. If your thing is prayer—wonderful. You have my support. . . . I appreciate them for who they are. I don't expect them to be what I want them to be. I appreciate them for being what the Church allows them to be.

In general, the bishops expressed an appreciation for the contributions of women religious, both as individuals and as congregations. A bishop from a midwestern diocese described the changing presence of women religious in his diocese:

> The thing about the religious sisters is they were willing to go to places that were small, had hardly any resources. The religious sisters down here—I think they would tell you—they had a great relationship with the priests, because down here . . . there's a lot of poverty. They didn't have much, what they had, they had the faith, they had a vision, and they worked hard, and so many of them will talk about the pastor and the sisters doing all this work together. There was a real comradery, and there's still a very strong sense of that. In our day and age, with the religious numbers having shrunk, but I'd say now they're in those key positions like at parishes where they're pastoral associates, working with the RCIA, working in the university, stuff like that. They may not have the visibility, but they have the impact.

Members of religious orders, women in particular, were some of the first people to start moving into positions formerly reserved for priests. In some ways they paved the way for lay people to follow. *Apostolicam Actusoitatem*[12] from Vatican II called for increased involvement of the laity

---

12. Second Vatican Council, "Decree on the Apostolate of the Laity: Apostolicam Actusitatem," November 18, 1965, http://www.vatican.va/archive/hist_councils/ii_vatican_council/documents/vat-ii_decree_19651118_apostolicam-actuositatem_en.html.

in the life of the Church, which directly fostered the movement of lay people into ministry.

Lay Ecclesial Ministers

In this section we focus on bishops' experiences with lay people who serve as professional Church ministers rather than the laity in general. According to Vatican II, the primary vocation of the laity is being "in the world." Ministry in the Church is the focus of ordained clergy, and to some extent, consecrated religious.[13] The decline in the number of religious brothers and sisters in Church positions corresponds with an increase in the presence of lay people in these positions. However, the number of lay ecclesial ministers has increased beyond just replacing retiring religious. The emergence of the term *lay ecclesial minister* acknowledges a growing presence of laity as professional Church ministers. As of 2014, lay people (who are not religious brothers or sisters) comprised about one-quarter of the professional workforce in the U.S. Catholic Church.[14] In 2005, the USCCB published a statement on lay ecclesial ministers as a resource for lay ministry development, *Co-Workers in the Vineyard of the Lord*. The bishops described lay ecclesial ministers as follows:

> By virtue of their call, lay ecclesial ministers take on a new relationship to the mission of the Church and to the other ministers who work to accomplish it. Therefore, they must be persons who are known for genuine love of the whole Catholic Church, who exist in full communion of heart and mind with the pope as successor of Peter, and whose ecclesial identity is shaped by obedience to the bishop of the diocese and to the universal magisterium and is expressed by generous collaboration with ordained and other lay ecclesial ministers alike.[15]

The USCCB continues to give attention to issues related to lay ecclesial ministry as evidenced by the 2015 summit convened to reflect on the prior

---

13. Ibid.

14. Center for Applied Research in the Apostolate, "Lay Ecclesial Ministers in the United States." Presentation at USCCB Lay Ecclesial Ministry Summit, July 7, 2015, St. Louis, MO.

15. United States Conference of Catholic Bishops, *Co-Workers*.

ten years, identify best practices in lay ecclesial ministry, and make recommendations for the future.[16]

In an interview, a retired bishop gave this perspective on lay ecclesial ministers:

> I think it's a very important ministry, and I think it is necessary for all of us to understand that not everybody is called to the clerical state or to religious life. These lay people bring a whole different perspective to ministry that we lack because they come from a marriage situation or a single situation, and they bring those insights into their service and into their dealings with clergy and religious. So we get an image of the entire Church by having lay ecclesial ministers serving with us.

When discussing the distinction between lay and ordained ministry, this bishop acknowledged the importance of clear boundaries and recognized the distinct roles of lay and ordained ministers. In reflecting on an experience with lay ecclesial ministers he gave this example:

> When I took over the diocese I created a position in the chancery for a lay person that was very similar to the work of a vicar general, but since that is a clerical title we had to be creative in the naming of the position. It was the duty of that person to oversee many of the ministries of the diocese, but without the title of vicar general.

This highlights an important distinction between functions and roles. The lay minister in this example may perform similar functions as a vicar general typically would, but still does not serve in the ecclesial role of vicar general—which is reserved for ordained ministers. The difference in title is significant and helps clarify the boundaries between lay and ordained ministry.

A common example of where lay ecclesial ministers serve in positions typically held by priests are Parish Life Coordinators—lay persons serving as pastoral leaders of parishes, with a priest assigned to provide sacramental ministry. We explore this further in the next chapter.

---

16. Richard J. Malone, "USCCB Lay Ecclesial Ministry Summit Report," Presentation at United States Conference of Catholic Bishops Lay Ecclesial Ministry Summit (St. Louis, MO, 2015).

Thus far we have discussed the different types of Church ministry personnel the bishop relates to—*who* the bishop works with. The next section explores *how* the bishop consults with others to govern and administer his diocese.

Consulting Bodies

In the interviews, several bishops elaborated on how they collaborate with others, particularly the different groups they rely on for consultation in decision making. The depth and detail of these reflections gives evidence that bishops do not make decisions in isolation, rather, they rely regularly on advisors and advisory groups. Commonly mentioned groups include the priests' council, some form of cabinet or group of chancery office heads, finance council, and priest personnel board. Some bishops also mentioned a diocesan pastoral council. A bishop from the Midwest summed up what he referred to as the "old standard bodies:"

> We have a diocesan pastoral council, I talk to consultors, the presbyteral council, and we have the finance council. All four of those meet regularly. Plus we have here at the curia a kind of a leadership team. We just did a couple of days on the amazing parish model for our leadership team. To deepen our sense of collaboration here.

A bishop from the South discussed a similar set of groups, highlighting his consistency in consulting these key advisory bodies:

> Groups that I speak with before any major decision is made are: (1) the presbyteral council, (2) the council of deans, (3) the ministerial council (which is made up of about 30 people who serve as chairs of every office), and (4) the administrative council, which is like a policy group. No major decision would be made without checking with those four groups. For example, we just finished a diocesan-wide synod. Any project in our moving forward with the implementation of the synod would have to be presented to all four of those groups.

Bishops mentioned the priests' council in a variety of different situations, emphasizing the bishops' relationships with the priests of their dioceses as key collaborators. One bishop shared:

[T]hrough our *[priests' council]* discussions of general themes for the diocese, we came to the conclusion that we needed to go through a process to develop a diocesan pastoral vision. . . . I think that came really as a challenge from the priests' council to me to articulate a vision in the diocese for the next several years. So I took the challenge seriously, but I decided it was probably better for me not just to do that on my own. We have a pretty good process to come to something that people seem to be rallying around.

Other bishops mentioned specific individuals in key advisory positions, such as the vicar general and the chief financial officer. For example, a bishop from a western diocese said:

I rely on the vicar general in the first place. He is a priest who has been here his entire life. Second, I look towards the priest personnel board for collaboration and advice, and finally our diocesan CFO who is truly an extraordinary human being. Not only is he very well trained in financial matters but he's a very good Catholic. Those are the three people or groups that I consult whenever I make a big decision.

A bishop from the Northeast gave some examples of how he relied on groups and individuals directly involved in a particular situation requiring a painful decision:

For every major decision, I would call in people from various offices who were responsible for the direction of different parts of the diocese. Say there's a discussion of whether or not we have to close a school. . . . It is always a painful thing. We would call in the finance people, we would call in the school office, the vicar general, the chancellor, the pastor, and the administrator of the school. We would have these sessions to discuss how we would try to reverse the trend or how we are going to handle the closure. I realized when I became a bishop that I did not have all the answers. I am not God. I needed to get input, collaboration, and insight, and I can't get it all by myself. You have to get it from the outside and from people who have the expertise to help make that decision.

A bishop's primary responsibility is to his local diocese, and he relies on a variety of personnel to assist him. However, bishops are also responsible together for the governance of the Church as a whole, particularly as expressed on a national level. The final section of this chapter explores bishops' relationships with each other, both on a personal level and considering other bishops as collaborators in ministry.

Relationships with Other Bishops

Friendships

In response to a survey question stating "other bishops are among my closest friends," 42 percent of bishops agreed "somewhat" and 27 percent agreed "strongly." In considering the influence of multiple bishop and diocesan characteristics, the only significant factor is that older bishops, specifically those from earlier priest ordination cohorts, are more likely to agree that other bishops are among their closest friends.

A bishop from a northeastern diocese gave a comprehensive commentary describing several things influencing his development of friendships with other bishops:

> I haven't found you get to know the bishops very well at those [USCCB] meetings. . . . I have bishop friends who are classmates I have known from the seminary for forty-five years. Others perhaps I have met along the way. So those you have known for a long time you still count them among your friends. I find it very difficult to create new friendships among other bishops simply because they are bishops. They come from different parts of the country, you don't know them very well and you have not studied with them. You have never worked with them closely. The fact that you are all bishops doesn't mean you are necessarily all friends. I think you might be coworkers, you have mutual respect, support, and admiration, but the friends that I have are those that I have known for a long time.

This quote helps clarify why priest ordination cohort perhaps matters more than length of time as a bishop. The possible comradery among bishops is based on an initial comradery among seminarians or other earlier relationships.

Collaboration in Ministry

The *Catechism of the Catholic Church* highlights an ordinary's dual responsibility for his local diocese as well as the broader Church:

> As Christ's vicar, each bishop has the pastoral care of the particular Church entrusted to him, but at the same time he bears collegially with all his brothers in the episcopacy the solicitude for all the Churches. Though each bishop is the lawful pastor only of the portion of the flock entrusted to his care, as a legitimate successor of the apostles he is, by divine institution and precept, responsible with the other bishops for the apostolic mission of the Church.[17]

National: United States Conference of Catholic Bishops (USCCB)

Vatican II called for the establishment of national episcopal conferences to foster collaboration among bishops.[18] The USCCB website provides a description of the Conference:

> The USCCB is an assembly of the hierarchy of the United States and the U.S. Virgin Islands who jointly exercise certain pastoral functions on behalf of the Christian faithful of the United States. The purpose of the Conference is to promote the greater good which the Church offers humankind, especially through forms and programs of the apostolate fittingly adapted to the circumstances of time and place.[19]

In the interviews, some bishops expressed mixed views about involvement in the USCCB and the Conference's influence or impact. For example, a bishop from the South said:

> I believe in the importance of the state and national level of the conferences. Sometimes the bureaucracy at the USCCB can be a

---

17. *Catechism of the Catholic Church*, No. 1560 (New York: Doubleday, 1995).

18. Second Vatican Council, *Decree Concerning the Pastoral Office of Bishops in the Church: Christus Dominus*, October 28, 1965, http://www.vatican.va/archive/hist_councils/ii_vatican_council/documents/vat-ii_decree_19651028_christus-dominus_en.html.

19. United States Conference of Catholic Bishops, "About USCCB." http://www.usccb.org/about/ (accessed July 9, 2017).

bit much; nonetheless, I believe in what it does and I believe in the mission of the Conference.

A bishop from the Midwest described his ambivalence:

On the Bishops' Conference I finished a three year term as chair of a committee for the Conference. I've tried to do my part; I've served on some other committees. I'm sort of ambivalent about the value of all that. I have to be frank. . . I think it's good, all things considered it's better for bishops to work together than not to. We're able to access the collaboration of a lot of other groups beyond the Conference and I've found that part to be interesting and kind of stimulating. . . . I think the Conference spends a lot of time issuing statements and having meetings and I don't know, I'm not sure anybody's paying attention. I don't think I'm cynical, I don't want to be, I'm just not sure if it's really, really meeting . . . or sort of helping to shape the discussion much or help move us forward.

When asked about his relationships with other bishops, a bishop from the West focused on interpersonal relationships and expressed disinterest with the USCCB, framed within his need to focus on the needs of his local diocese:

I have three bishop friends that I can call for advice and I often do that. There are others with whom I am "friendly" but not really that close. I find the other levels you mentioned very bureaucratic. I don't want to be on any committee for the USCCB and so I am not. I have a lot of work to do here in this diocese and I am alone.

Although several bishops expressed concern or disinterest in the USCCB, the bishops do participate in the semi-annual meeting, and some participate more actively through committees.

The work of the USCCB is conducted by staff offices and by a variety of committees that bishops serve on. In addition to these standing committees, temporary committees reflect the bishops' focus on current issues.

Half of the active Latin Rite ordinaries serve on at least one committee. Of the 128 bishops serving on USCCB committees (including Latin Rite ordinaries, auxiliaries, retired bishops, and Eastern Rite eparchs), 81 serve on one committee, 31 serve on two, and 15 serve on three or four. One bishop sits on five committees.

One example of the work of USCCB ad hoc committees is *The Charter for the Protection of Children and Young People*, part of the U.S. bishops' response to the sex abuse scandals. "The charter addresses the Church's commitment to deal appropriately and effectively with cases of sexual abuse of minors by priests, deacons, and other church personnel."[20] It includes directions for dioceses and eparchies to have policies and procedures to respond to allegations, standards for behavior, a victim's assistance coordinator, a review board, establish safe environment programs, and engage in an annual audit reviewing compliance with the norms and procedures.

The *Charter* also includes a *Statement of Episcopal Commitment* developed by the Ad Hoc Committee on Bishops' Life and Ministry. The statement acknowledges individual bishops' autonomy but emphasizes the "collegiality and fraternity" and the bishops' responsibility to "protect the unity and promote the common discipline of the whole Church."[21] After the retirement of Bishop Bruskewitz in 2015, all 178 Latin Rite dioceses have accepted the *Charter* and are committed to complying with the annual audit and reporting. However, a few bishops who committed to the *Charter* have been critiqued for failing to fully comply.[22]

Another example of the joint work of bishops through the USCCB is *Forming Consciences for Faithful Citizenship*. This document provides "guidance for Catholics in the exercise of their rights and duties as participants in our democracy."[23] A committee formed to revise the document prior to the 2016 election was composed of chairmen from ten of

20. United States Conference of Catholic Bishops, *Charter for the Protection of Children and Young People* (Washington, DC, 2018), http://www.usccb.org/issues-and-action/child-and-youth-protection/upload/Charter-for-the-Protection-of-Children-and-Young-People-2018.pdf.

21. Ibid.

22. Michael Sean Winters, "The Dallas Charter is on Life-Support." *The National Catholic Reporter*, June 2, 2011, https://www.ncronline.org/blogs/distinctly-catholic/dallas-charter-life-support.

23. United States Conference of Catholic Bishops, *Forming Consciences for Faithful Citizenship: A Call to Political Responsibility from the Catholic Bishops of the United States with Introductory Note* (Washington, DC, 2015), http://www.usccb.org/issues-and-action/faithful-citizenship/forming-consciences-for-faithful-citizenship-title.cfm.

the USCCB committees.[24] The USCCB accepted the revisions by a vote of 210 in favor, 21 opposed, and five abstentions. This was a clear majority, but not unanimous. The debate over the document highlights tensions among the bishops. Some bishops called for a new document, rather than just a revision—a document taking more into account the priorities of Pope Francis. The support for the revised rather than new document referenced the "hermeneutic of continuity," a term associated more with Pope Benedict XI.[25]

State Catholic Conferences

State Catholic Conferences can be a forum for collaboration among bishops within a state. Out of the 50 states and the District of Columbia, 43 have a Catholic Conference. Most of the states without a Conference are composed of a single diocese. However, eight single-state dioceses still have a State Catholic Conference. These single-diocese conferences do not provide the same opportunity for collaboration among bishops, but they focus on addressing state-level policy and legislative issues and engage in lobbying efforts, so they need to be organizationally separate from the diocese.

A retired bishop contrasted his participation in the national and state conferences:

> In my younger days I was more involved with the USSCB. As I was aging I knew that my tenure was coming to an end and so I withdrew more and more. However, I was always very involved on a state level with different issues, like statute of limitations and similar topics. I just felt it was very critical to be involved at that level. We had four quarterly meetings every year. And with the use of cell

---

24. Catholic Education, Communications, Cultural Diversity in the Church, Doctrine, Domestic Justice and Human Development, Evangelization and Catechesis, International Justice and Peace, Migration, Pro-Life Activities; the Subcommittee for the Promotion and Defense of Marriage; and the Ad Hoc Committee for Religious Liberty.

25. Matthew Brunson, "Recap of USCCB Assembly Day 2: Debating Faithful Citizenship," *Our Sunday Visitor Weekly*, November 18, 2015, https://www.osv.com/OSVNewsweekly/Article/TabId/535/ArtMID/13567/ArticleID/18734/Recap-of-USCCB-assembly-Day-2-Debating-faithful-citizenship.aspx;

Tom Roberts, "Bishops Pass 'Faithful Citizenship,' Some Call for New Document," *National Catholic Reporter*, November 17, 2015, https://www.ncronline.org/news/vatican/us-bishops-pass-revised-faithful-citizenship-some-call-new-document.

phones and other technology we could keep in touch with each other constantly.

When asked if he spoke out on public issues, a bishop from the South responded:

No. Because most of that, to be very honest with you, was done through the State Bishops' Conference. . . . I've never done it on my own because we've all always done it together. And I've never had anything that only affected this diocese or this state. It's always been affecting more than this diocese so the State Conference, we all take a stand together at that time.

State Conferences are forums for bishops to write joint statements on issues active in the state legislature such as gay marriage, euthanasia, and immigration. Chapter 7 will explore the bishop's role as teacher, providing guidance to Church members on spiritual, moral, and social issues. The next chapter continues the discussion of the bishops' role in governance and administration.

6

Governance and Administration

When you become the diocesan bishop, then everything stops at your desk and at your door. You have that great responsibility for shepherding a diocese and that responsibility is spiritual, it's canonical, it's legal. All those worlds are something you are responsible for. . . . These [roles] are all the bishop. They are all that any pastor has defined, those three ways: of teaching, of governing, and of sanctifying. That is the role of any bishop or any pastor, through [to] the Pope. It's actually the role of Jesus: to teach, to govern, and to sanctify, so it would be hard to say any one of those is more important than the other. They really do complement each other and they work well together and you really cannot separate one out over the other. They are all equal parts of the challenge and the privilege of shepherding a Church.

BISHOP OF A NORTHEASTERN DIOCESE

It's different because when I was a pastor in a parish I had to deal, for the most part, with problems of my own making. A bishop has to deal with problems of someone else's making.

BISHOP FROM A SOUTHERN DIOCESE

Well, now people look to me for the vision.

BISHOP REFLECTING ON HIS CHANGE IN ROLE
FROM AUXILIARY BISHOP TO ORDINARY

THIS CHAPTER DISCUSSES the bishop's governance and administrative role and explores three areas of diocesan administration: (1) strategies for parish leadership staffing, given the possibly limited number of available priests; (2) diocesan pastoral and strategic planning; and (3) policies for key aspects of Church life that are legislated at the diocesan level.

This chapter takes the perspective of the diocese as an organization and the bishop as the leader and administrator of that organization. In business terms the bishop would be the chief executive officer. A diocese is perhaps more comparable to a nonprofit organization, where the CEO is the administrator and the board of directors are responsible for governance and mission. However, in the case of the diocese, the bishop is responsible for both the administration and governance.

In political governance terms, the bishop might be thought of as head of the executive branch, but there is no separation of powers in Church governance. Canon law states: "it is for the diocesan bishop to govern the particular church entrusted to him with legislative, executive, and judicial power according to the norm of law." Therefore, the bishop has authority over all three elements of governance.[1]

Analogies from the business, nonprofit, and political fields give some insight into the role of the bishop by comparing him to leaders of other familiar organizations. However, it is important to identify the distinctive nature of Church governance and leadership. The bishop is not the CEO or president, but the pastor of the local (diocesan) Church. The first quote at the beginning of the chapter emphasizes the ecclesial and pastoral nature of the bishop's leadership role—to be, as Jesus is, priest, prophet, and king. The second quote highlights the fact that while a parish priest also fulfills these three roles, the diocesan bishop governs at a higher level in the organizational structure of the Church. He has less direct influence at the local parish level, but he still has the overall responsibility for what happens at the local level. The third quote provides an important context for the first quote. While the bishop is responsible for a variety of administrative and governance responsibilities, as the shepherd of the diocese and as primarily a spiritual leader, providing a vision is perhaps his most important role. The broader context of this last quote is that as an auxiliary bishop, he saw his role as supporting the vision of the ordinary, whereas as an ordinary himself, the vision is his responsibility.

---

1. The Canon Law Society of America, *Code of Canon Law*, no. 391.1 (Washington, DC: Liberia Editrice Vaticana, 2003), http://www.vatican.va/archive/ENG1104/_INDEX.HTM).

The Bishop as Administrator

The survey included an open-ended question asking the bishops to list their three most important roles. The bishops commonly responded in terms of the traditional characterization of the elements of Christ's priesthood—priest, prophet, and king.[2] They did not typically use these specific titles, but more often described the roles in terms of sanctifying/worship, teaching/preaching, and leading/governing. Combining the bishops' three responses, 80 percent identified the teaching role, 63 percent mentioned sanctifying, and 55 percent listed administrative. In response to an interview question asking about their most important role, bishops consistently put the teaching and sanctifying roles above administration. However, as Chapter 4 discussed, 43 percent of bishops responded that "organizing and administering the work of the Church" was of "great" importance in terms of satisfaction.

An important example of a bishop's administrative responsibility is assigning priests to parish leadership as pastors. This includes deciding how to provide parish leadership when there is a limited number of available priests, or shifts in population leave some parishes under-utilized or create areas of the diocese that are under-served.

Strategies for Parish Leadership Staffing

The survey included two questions about potential problems bishops experience related to parish staffing. Over half (52 percent) of the bishops described the limited number of available priests as "a great" problem. An additional one-third (34 percent) reported it was "somewhat" of a problem. Only 14 percent said it was "little" or "no" problem. When asked about parish restructuring, 40 percent of bishops reported it was either "somewhat" or "a great" problem. Bishops' experiences with these two issues are related. Bishops who perceived the limited number of available priests as being a problem were also more likely to identify parish restructuring as a problem.

Bishops have adopted several strategies for addressing parish leadership needs in the face of a limited number of available priests, including increasing vocation efforts, appointing one priest as pastor for multiple parishes, increasing the use of international priests, closing or merging

---

2. *Catechism of the Catholic Church*, no. 436 (New York: Doubleday, 1995).

parishes, use of non-priests as parish leaders, and increasing the priest retirement age.

Figure 6.1 shows the change between 1986 and 2015 in the percentage of dioceses using some of these different strategies. Dioceses with more than 5 percent of parishes having a nonresident pastor rose steadily from 31 percent in 1986 to 71 percent in 2015. Dioceses that used parish life coordinators went from 30 percent in 1986 to a peak of 57 percent in 2003, and declined to 43 percent in 2015. Increased use of extern priests and parish closings both show a jagged, up and down pattern. Increase in extern priests peaked at 47 percent of dioceses, and parish closings at 38 percent.

Bishops responded to two sets of survey questions about the use of different parish leadership staffing strategies: the extent to which they had used different strategies in the past five years, and how likely they would be to use these strategies in the future. Table 6.1 displays the results for both sets of questions. For each strategy, the first row shows the last five years and the second row shows the next five years.

The percentages for the 2015 OCD data (Figure 6.1) are fairly consistent with the responses to the survey questions about the use of these strategies in the last five years. The OCD measures for increases in seminarians

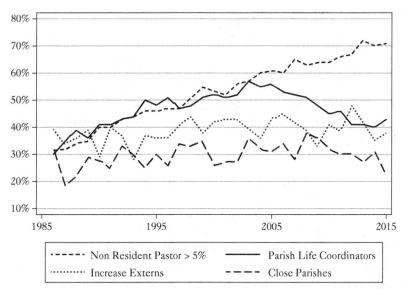

FIGURE 6.1 Percentage of Dioceses Using Different Strategies to Address Parish Leadership Staffing

Source: Official Catholic Directory, 1986–2015.

Table 6.1 Strategies to Address the Limited Number of
Available Priests to Lead Parishes

Extent Used in Last 5 Years	Not at All (%)	Not Very Much (%)	Somewhat (%)	A Fair Amount (%)
Increase vocations	1	3	21	75
One priest multiple parishes	9	19	31	42
Increase international priests	13	26	37	24
Close/merge parishes	46	25	18	11
Non-priest led parishes	57	18	21	5
Increase priest retirement age	68	16	11	4
Willingness in Next 5 years	Not Likely at All (%)	Not Very Likely (%)	Somewhat Likely (%)	Very Likely (%)
Increase vocations	1	0	10	90
One priest multiple parishes	6	16	34	44
Increase international priests	13	31	42	14
Close/merge parishes	26	32	28	14
Non-priest led parishes	32	25	28	15
Increase priest retirement age	50	35	10	6

Source: CARA Survey of Bishops, 2016.

and increases in extern priests are notably lower than the survey results for increased vocation efforts and increased use of international priests. This is likely because the OCD categories are proxy measures for what was directly asked in the survey. We discuss details from Table 6.1 in the following sections on each of the strategies.

Increasing Vocation Efforts

It is reasonable to assume that all bishops have in place ongoing efforts to encourage vocations to the priesthood, so the survey question was specifically phrased to focus on "increasing" efforts as a strategy to address the limited number of available priests. This was the most frequently reported strategy, both for the last five years and for the next five. Given the high response level, it is possible the bishops interpreted the question to be about vocation efforts in general, rather than specifically increasing their efforts.

There is a notable shift from 75 percent reporting "a fair amount" of use in the last five years to 90 percent being "very willing" in the next five years.

There are some differences among bishops based on theological orientation. For the past five years, moderate bishops were more likely than traditional bishops to have increased vocation efforts "a fair amount." There were no significant differences between moderate and liberal bishops or between traditional and liberal bishops. Some research has suggested that more traditionally-oriented dioceses are associated with higher numbers of seminarians.[3] It is possible that traditional bishops have been focusing on vocations for some time and, therefore, have not necessarily increased their efforts in the last five years. Moderate bishops may have more recently seen the need to increase their efforts.

Looking ahead to the next five years, bishops from the younger priest ordination cohorts (post-Vatican II and millennial) are more likely than the older cohorts to be "very willing" to focus on increasing vocations to the priesthood. The analysis controlled for theological orientation and length of time in the diocese. Therefore, it is not the case that the younger cohorts focus on vocations because they are possibly more traditional, or that newer bishops are starting up increased efforts. It seems simply to be that younger bishops are more likely than older bishops to increase vocation efforts (or focus on vocations).

An interview question asked bishops to look five to ten years ahead about balancing the number of Catholics and parishes with the number of available priests. Several bishops emphasized the importance of this strategy. For example, one bishop said:

> Well I must say, happily, that we are in pretty good shape. Last year we had six ordinations. We have forty-four seminarians and so all of our parishes are covered. Now, the problem is, you don't always have the right personalities and the right gifts to cover them, but we are not lacking in personnel at this point.

This quote highlights the interconnectedness of the issues bishops deal with. It is not enough to have a strong vocation program, resulting in enough seminarians and new priests. Having enough priests to lead

3. Rodney Stark and Roger Finke, "Catholic Religious Vocations: Decline and Renewal," *Review of Religious Research* 45, no. 2 (2000): 125–145.

all the parishes also requires "the right personalities," or a lack of priest personnel problems.

Another bishop included women religious in his response about vocation efforts:

> We have set up a program where we are asking for names of men and women who may be called to religious life or priesthood. Also, we have a house of discernment for women who are thinking about religious life and they can live there. We sponsor it by providing the house and all that is needed to run it. We expect religious congregations of women to staff it and work with it. I don't know if too many dioceses have something like that for women religious. We have some "Come and See" dinners throughout the year. The young men come for a meal, they pray a little, and then have a talk on vocations. Also, I have created a vocations committee made up of many younger priests. None of them are old enough to be a director of vocations but they are good encouragers. A couple of them are really good at it.

Having enough local, new recruits to the priesthood is the clear preference for the bishops, with 100 percent of them focusing on vocation efforts into the next five years. However, the bishops also recognize that vocation efforts are not enough, and they need to use other strategies to manage parish leadership staffing.

One Priest for Multiple Parishes

"Because of lack of priests or other circumstances" (Can. 526.1), a bishop can assign one priest as pastor to multiple parishes. Multiple-parish pastoring is not new, but recent research indicates the practice is growing and is now the most frequently used nontraditional model. The size and number of parishes a single pastor is responsible for may also be growing.[4]

Related to this is a parish clustering strategy. Canon 517.1 allows a team of priests to pastor several parishes. For example, three priests might jointly pastor four or more parishes.

---

4. Mark Mogilka and Kate Wiskus, *Pastoring Multiple Parishes* (Chicago: Loyola Press, 2009).

Having one priest as pastor for multiple parishes was the second most common strategy for both the last five years and the next five years. About three-quarters of the bishops responded they had used this strategy "some" or "a fair amount" in the last five years. Looking ahead, there is only a 5 percent anticipated increase in the higher use responses "somewhat" or "very" willing.

For the past five years, bishops who identified the limited number of available priests as "a great" problem were more likely to use the strategy of one pastor for multiple parishes a "fair amount." Bishops with shorter tenure were also more likely to use this strategy. This could be because it is a strategy that can be implemented more quickly. Bishops in the Midwest were more likely than bishops in the other regions to have used the multiple-parish pastoring. This might be related to population shifts, but the Northeast—which is experiencing similar population downsizing— does not show the same dynamic.

For the next five years, greater concern about a limited number of available priests and shorter tenure in the diocese continue to influence greater expected use of this strategy. Bishops from the Midwest are more likely than those in the South to rely "a fair amount" on having one priest for multiple parishes.

One bishop gave an example illustrating how a clustering strategy addresses multiple needs. He recognized that priests being able to work and live together is a benefit for the Church, yet he also recognized that the traditional multiple-priest parish is still the desired norm:

> I have been, and I want to continue to, cluster, preferably merge parishes, not necessarily closing anything, but then give the pastor an associate so they can live together and work together and handle things that way. Diocesan priests I know were ordained primarily to serve a parish and would be by themselves, but if I can get away from the lone ranger attitude and get more a sense of cooperation among the priests I think that's a benefit to the Church and the parishes as well. Now the downside of this is that the place [parish] where the priest does not live, they often feel like second class citizens or they feel like they are not attracting the attention they should get. I understand that, too. The parishes are a place where you have a father of the family gather them together to worship and to care for one another. So, I understand that value as well. This is a time that I think we need to do some more experimentation.

This bishop's reflection discussed the benefits and limitations of this strategy and recognized the importance of meeting the needs of both priests and parishioners.

Rather than trying to stretch his priest resources, a bishop may try to increase the number of priests by recruiting priests from other countries.

Increased Use of International Priests

The third most common strategy in the last five years was increasing the use of international priests. Bishops were less likely to mention this strategy for the next five years—it drops to fourth on the list. This could be a reflection of the problems encountered in working with international priests that were discussed in Chapter 5. There is no change in the percentage of bishops who are "not at all" willing to increase the use of international priests, but there is a consistent drop in the other response categories, showing a general decrease in willingness to use this strategy.

Bishops with a greater concern about the limited number of available priests are more likely to report increased use of international priests, both in the past five years and for the next five years. In the past five years, bishops from the West were more likely than those in the Midwest to have increased their number of international priests. It may be that the greater cultural diversity of the population in the West is a better fit for more international priests. There are no regional differences looking ahead five years.

The bishop quoted earlier, saying he was in "pretty good shape" with the priest–parish balance, acknowledged his reliance on foreign priests:

> It wouldn't be possible without them. Of course, we do not have enough native Hispanic priests. We also, because of our location, have a lot of Vietnamese priests, a lot. But, they came here after the fall of Vietnam, so they were parishioners here that became priests. And then we have a growing number of Africans.

This response distinguishes between foreign-born priests who are part of a broader immigrant community and priests who are recruited from other countries or regions. His reference to the need for "native Hispanic priests" raises a question about whether the issue is one of domestic versus international priests, or if it is a matter of having priests who are able to "fit in" with the culture of the parish community. This is especially relevant given the increasing ethnic diversity of the Catholic population.

If increasing the number of available priests—either through vocation efforts or by recruiting international priests—is not enough to bridge the possible gap between number of priests and number of parishes, bishops need to consider other options.

Closing or Merging Parishes

For the last five years, 29 percent of bishops reported closing or merging parishes "somewhat" or "a fair amount." It was the fourth most common response, with basically the same level of support as using non-priests. These two strategies are at half the level of using international priests. Overall, there is a notable increase for the next five years in plans for closing/merging parishes, with 42 percent of bishops reporting they plan on doing this "somewhat" or "a fair amount." Bishops show a 20 percent shift from "not used at all" in the last five years to either "not very" or "somewhat" willing, in the next five years, with little increase in the number who are "very" willing. Plans to use non-priests increased at the same rate, so use of these strategies remained similar.

Similar factors influenced the likelihood of closing or merging parishes for both the past five years and the next five years. Again, greater concern about limited available priests is a significant influence. Bishops from more populous dioceses were more likely to report closing/merging parishes as a common strategy. Regional differences again reflect the demographic shift in population from the Northeast and Midwest to the South and West. In the past five years, bishops in the Midwest were more likely than either those in the South or West to close or merge parishes. In the next five years, closures in the Midwest and Northeast are more likely than in the South.

A Midwestern bishop recognized the challenge to balance pastoral needs with the more rational assessment based on numbers. His commentary suggests that demographic shifts, rather than the limited number of priests, are the rationale for possible parish closures:

The question is, do we need all these parishes and missions down here and the answer is no. I have one mission that has seven families. It's pure sentimentality that keeps the priest coming there. He doesn't want to be the one who says, "no I'm not going to come." But after him I don't know if a new priest that replaces him decides "I can't do this." I can't fault him. Do we need all our current parishes and missions? I'll be the first to say no, we don't. I would rather that realization come from the people. And even if we had enough clergy, do we really need to stay open, with modern modes of transportation? Even though we're a rural diocese, nobody comes to Mass by horse and buggy any more. Everybody has a car. And that's the reality and given that transportation shift we don't need all these missions, but we'll keep them until . . . I would like someday these small missions to wake up and say "you know we had a good run of it, we're just not needed any more."

This reflection emphasizes a pastoral, rather than utilitarian approach to leadership and decision making. This bishop may well be able to make the difficult decision to close a parish or mission, but his response suggests a desire to exercise subsidiarity by allowing the decision to come from the priests and parishioners.

Non-Priest Parish Leader

Canon law allows a bishop to entrust a parish to a non-priest.

If, because of a lack of priests, the diocesan bishop has decided that participation in the exercise of the pastoral care of a parish is to be entrusted to a deacon, to another person who is not a priest, or to a community of persons, he is to appoint some priest who, provided with the powers and faculties of a pastor, is to direct the pastoral care.[5]

Although the use of canon 517.2 is contingent upon there being a lack of priests, it is the bishop who decides if there is a lack of priests. The bishop appoints a non-priest parish life coordinator (PLC) to be the day-to-day leader of the parish and serve all leadership functions except the sacramental roles, which only an ordained minister can perform.

For both the past five years and next five years, using non-priests has the same level of support as closing/merging parishes (based on combining "somewhat" and "fair amount," and "somewhat willing" and "very willing"). However, using non-priests increased from 5 percent of the bishops using this strategy "a fair amount" in the last five years to

5. The Canon Law Society of America, *Code of Canon Law*, no. 517.2.

15 percent being "very willing" to use it in the next five years. It moves from the fifth most common strategy to the third most common. Figure 6.1 shows a steady decline in the number of dioceses using non-priests to lead parishes between 2005 and 2015. However, the survey responses suggest that looking ahead to the next five years, using non-priest leaders is the strategy that is likely to show the greatest increase in use. There is only a 10 percent anticipated increase in the number of bishops who plan on using non-priest leaders "a fair amount," but there is a 25 percent decrease in the number of bishops who are "not at all willing" to consider this strategy.

Looking back over the past five years, over half (57 percent) of the bishops reported using non-priest personnel "not at all." This is consistent with data from Figure 6.1 which shows the percentage of dioceses using PLCs nationwide has been declining since 2003, and decreased from 46 percent in 2011 to 40 percent in 2014. In 2015, there was a slight increase to 43 percent. When asked about their plans for the next five years, only 32 percent of the bishops said they would be "not at all willing" to use PLCs. This suggests that the use of PLCs may again trend upward.

In the past five years, bishops from dioceses with larger populations were more likely to use non-priest leaders, but diocese size does not have an effect for the next five years. Theological orientation has a consistent effect—both in the past and looking ahead—with progressive bishops being more likely than moderates or traditional bishops to have used, or be willing to use, non-priest leaders.

A bishop from a Midwestern diocese gave an example of using deacons to lead parishes and also emphasized the temporary nature of this strategy:

> We have four permanent deacons who are temporary administrators in parishes. I appreciate that they bring a real skill set that many priests do not have, obviously. They run businesses and things like that. I do notice that they are lacking—and I want to be careful about this—they cannot be the father of the family. They cannot fill that role and I am not quite sure why that is the case. I don't know whether it's on the part of the laity—they only will look to the priests to be the father of the family—or the deacons themselves don't identify with that. Of course they wouldn't because they weren't ordained to the priesthood. But, I do this kind of arrangement. Administrators are in parishes awaiting a pastor. That is the way I look at it.

Another bishop highlighted an important distinction between the number of priests and the number of *available* priests, and is clear about not wanting to use PLCs:

> We have too many parishes in places where the people have already moved away. I do not like the term "closure" and so we speak about mergers, not closures. As to the strategies we will follow, we will have a few more mergers. In some cases it is not that I don't have enough priests but that I don't have enough who can be pastors. Some of our priests just do the bare minimum. They celebrate Mass and then go to their rooms for the rest of the day. I don't believe in having parishes run by the laity. I inherited some parishes like that but we reassigned that situation a while ago. What I could see working in the future would be to have a priest as a spiritual leader of a parish and have a lay leader serve as the business manager. But that can be a difficult situation. In the past we've had a few places where the layperson in charge was bossing the priest around.

In 2007, CARA conducted a series of focus groups with bishops reflecting on their experiences after twenty years of using PLCs. Some bishops commented that what was intended as a temporary solution was in danger of becoming permanent. This concern is evident in the trend of PLC use over time. The number of PLCs in the United States grew to a peak of 556 in 2005 and declined to 343 by 2015. The focus groups also indicated that bishops might prefer deacons for PLCs, because they are ordained ministers and can perform some of the sacramental ministries.[6]

Figure 6.2 shows trends over time in the different types of parish life coordinators: deacons, brothers, sisters, and lay people. These follow trends similar to the numbers of these types of ministers in general. There is a decline in the number of sisters; brothers represent a stable but very minimal number; and there is an increase in the number of deacons and lay people. However, lay people have declined from their peak in 2005, while deacons continue to grow and now represent the largest number of PLCs.

Table 6.2 shows responses to the survey question, "In the absence of an available priest, how do you feel about appointing the following [types of personnel] to lead parishes?" At least 50 percent of bishops are either

6. Mary L. Gautier, Tricia C. Bruce, and Mary E. Bendyna, *Listening to the Spirit: Bishops and Parish Life Coordinators* (Washington, DC, 2007).

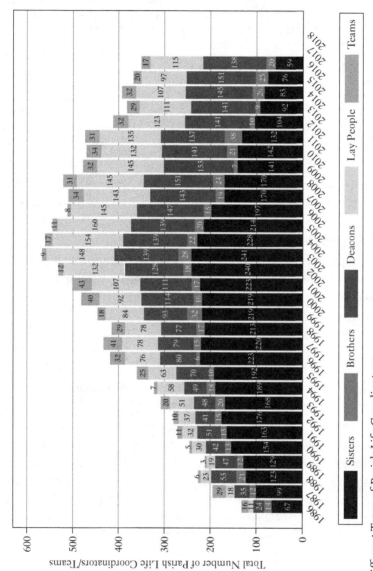

FIGURE 6.2 Different Types of Parish Life Coordinators

Source: *Official Catholic Directory*, 1986–2015.

Table 6.2 Willingness to Use a Non-Priest to Lead Parishes
in the Absence of an Available Priest

Personnel Type	Not at All Willing (%)	Not Very Willing (%)	Somewhat Willing (%)	Very Willing (%)
Permanent deacon	2	12	23	62
Religious sister	11	32	26	31
Religious brother	12	35	23	30
Lay woman	20	30	24	26
Lay man	19	31	25	25

Source: CARA Survey of Bishops, 2016.

"somewhat" or "very" willing to use any of the non-priest personnel. However, bishops are much more likely to be "very" willing to use deacons compared to religious or lay persons, and there appears to be some preference for religious brothers and sisters over lay men and women.

There is no effect of theological orientation on bishops' willingness to use deacons, but moderate and progressive bishops are more likely than traditional bishops to be willing to use religious or lay persons to lead parishes.

Increase Priest Retirement Age

Increasing the retirement age for priests was the least common strategy, with only 15 percent of bishops reporting "somewhat" or "a fair amount" of use in the past five years. Looking to the next five years, raising the priest retirement age remains the least popular choice, with 16 percent of bishops being "somewhat" or "very" willing. However, there is a 20 percent shift from "not at all" to only "not very" willing. This suggests that, however unpopular a choice, some bishops recognized they might need to consider it. There are no significant differences among bishop or diocesan characteristics regarding prior or intended future use of this strategy.

Multiple Strategies and Other Strategies

When asked in an interview about vocation efforts, one bishop recognized that relying on local vocations to the priesthood had never been enough, so he discussed multiple strategies:

We are only ordaining [new priests] two or three every other year and we are striving to do that. We have a new vocations director and he is working at it. But we have to be realistic, even if we get again, three or say two a year, we are not going to satisfy all that we have to serve by our own native population. The diocese has never done that. In the past the Irish came. At a certain point in [this state] half the priests are from Ireland. They are fading obviously— the youngest is sixty-five. There is not a boatload coming over from Ireland anytime soon. . . . At the same time we are holding steady with the priest situation. We have lay ecclesial ministers, we call them by another name, pastoral ministers, where they are the ones in the parish day in and day out and a sacramental minister comes by and overall there's a canonical pastor who rarely has to get involved unless there is some issue. But we have had lay ecclesial ministers for the last thirty years here and they worked well overall.

The survey responses looking back five years also show evidence that bishops are using multiple strategies. About one-third (32 percent) of the bishops reported having two strategies they used "a fair amount" and 20 percent used three or four strategies "a fair amount." Including bishops who reported "some" use, 61 percent had three or more strategies.

A retired bishop reflected on additional—perhaps less conventional— possibilities:

The present Holy Father has said that if a national conference of bishops asks for a married clergy that he would consider that. We've noticed a few rumblings from Brazil and Germany but, to be frank, there has been nothing from our Conference. . . . I think we have to look at a married clergy. A married clergy will not be the end all and be all, but I think that we should look in to it as a possibility. We could have a part-time clergy and a full-time clergy. We need a whole new different approach. Parish leadership could be handled by the laity. I am also encouraged that the Vatican is looking in to the issue of women deacons now. I understand that some people think that such a change will lead to women priests. I think that one of the worst things that we did was to accept the Pastoral Provision guys. It is very much a double standard to allow them to serve but to not allow our guys to be married.

Pastoral Provision priests are Episcopalian or Anglican priests who convert to Roman Catholicism. If they are already married they can remain married. A bishop can choose whether or not to accept these priests, but the numbers are relatively small, so "recruiting" them would not be a very likely systematic strategy.

Allowing for married clergy, in general, is not currently a choice available to individual Latin Rite bishops, but as this bishop states, it is something the USCCB could request for the Holy Father to "consider."

In response to an interview question about the balance of priests and parishes and possible diocesan reconfiguration plans, several bishops mentioned that substantial reconfiguration had been addressed by their predecessor and that current planning was more pastorally focused. Others recognized the need to assess parish configurations but also focused on a more generally mission-oriented process. This connects the bishops' decision making about parish staffing to broader areas of diocesan leadership, such as diocesan pastoral planning.

Diocesan Planning Processes

Developing and implementing a diocesan pastoral plan is an important example of how a bishop exercises broad leadership in the diocese. The number of pastoral plans found on diocesan websites gives evidence that pastoral planning is a common practice. Out of the 178 Latin Rite diocese websites, 113 of them (64 percent) make reference to a pastoral plan, strategic plan, synod, or pastoral priorities within the last ten years. Descriptions of the planning processes indicated they generally included consultation with different groups, input from multiple constituencies, and often involved listening sessions throughout the diocese.

The common priorities listed in Table 6.3 confirm the pastoral orientation of these plans. "Catechesis, faith formation, and discipleship" was the most common response, included in almost half (48 percent) of the plans. Parish restructuring (41 percent) is almost as common as evangelization (42 percent). Although vocation efforts ranked high on the list of bishops' strategies for responding to a limited number of priests, only one-fifth (20 percent) of the diocesan plans included vocation efforts. It may be that bishops recognize or articulate this as a priority more so than members of the diocese in general.

Pastoral plans generally include action items that result in the development of new programs or increased attention or effort directed at

Table 6.3 Goals of Diocesan Pastoral Plans, Strategic Plans, Synods, and Capital Campaigns

	Pastoral Plan (%)	Capital Campaign (%)
Catechesis, faith formation, discipleship	48	26
Evangelization	42	17
Parish staffing, parish restructuring	41	
Worship, sacraments, and liturgy	32	
Outreach, social services, social justice	30	63
Youth, young adults	25	29
Family and marriage	24	
Vocations	20	
Education, Catholic schools (tuition assistance)	19	66
Stewardship	18	
Leadership (lay leader formation)	17	12
Administration or finance	13	
Spirituality	12	
Individual parish needs	11	65
Cultural diversity	10	
Clergy health and retirement		65
Seminary education support		57
Cathedral renovation		25
Other building renovations		25

Eight pastoral plans did not have clear goals, so the percentages are based on 106 dioceses. Capital campaign percentages are based on 66 dioceses.

Source: Diocesan Websites, 2017.

existing programs. These endeavors often require monetary resources to support them. A capital campaign is typically a fundraising effort directed at developing a building project of some kind. While some dioceses do have building or renovation projects, bishops are also using diocesan capital campaigns to raise funds for implementing elements of the pastoral plans. About one-third (35 percent) of dioceses with a pastoral plan also had a capital campaign.

Over one-third (37 percent) of dioceses engaged in a capital campaign within the last ten years. The areas of focus show common patterns among dioceses. Table 6.3 also shows the most frequently mentioned capital campaign goals. There is an overlap with pastoral planning goals, including

Catholic education, parish needs, service outreach, faith formation, evangelization, and leadership formation. There are, of course, some building projects. One-quarter of all capital campaigns included renovating the cathedral, and one-quarter had building projects other than the cathedral.

In an interview, a bishop spoke about how the initiative to develop a pastoral plan came from his priests' council:

> Through our [priests' council] discussions of general themes for the diocese we came to the conclusion that we needed to go through a process to develop a diocesan pastoral vision. I think that came really as a challenge from the priests' council to me to articulate a vision in the diocese for the next several years. So I took the challenge seriously, but I decided it was probably better for me not just to do that on my own. We have a pretty good process to come to something that people seem to be rallying around. . . . I got the help of the Catholic Leadership Institute in Philadelphia to work with some of our diocesan leadership to put together a process to be able to articulate a vision of what we would more like to resemble over the next 3–5 years.

A recently appointed bishop described how he is building upon the pastoral planning done by his predecessor:

> And one of the first groups I met with was the Visioning Committee that worked with the bishop down here. And I just thought it would be unfair—and actually in a sense unnecessary—to just throw that vision out and start over. Because I think that would really have stopped the direction in the diocese. I think there was a great momentum built around that vision. . . . And so I made the conscious choice. People said to me when I first came, what is your vision? And I said, my vision is I'm going to embrace the vision of this diocese. That is going to be my vision. My vision is your vision. I didn't feel like it was my right, in a sense, to maybe ignore all the work that had gone into forming this beautiful vision. Now, that's not to say maybe three to five years down the road I can put my twist on it, that's fine.

The USCCB developed its own 2017–2020 strategic plan. Priorities included five major themes: evangelization, marriage and family life, human life and dignity, vocations, and religious freedom. Some common themes are evident between the USCCB plan and individual diocesan plans such as evangelization, marriage and family, and vocations. Some of the USCCB priorities included sub-themes that are major themes in the diocesan plans. For example, the USCCB human life and dignity priority includes poverty and justice issues, which is comparable to the service and outreach in diocesan plans. Youth are included in the USCCB evangelization priority. The common elements between diocesan plans and the USCCB plan suggest some collaboration, interaction, or exchanging of ideas between bishops regarding pastoral priorities.

Religious freedom is a priority in the USCCB plan, but this was not included in any individual diocesan plan from the website review. This may be because it is an issue more appropriately dealt with on the national or state conference levels. In contrast, "catechesis, formation, and discipleship" is the most commonly listed priority in diocesan plans but is not a theme on the USCCB level. This may be because these efforts are more likely implemented on local diocesan levels.

Planning initiatives are occasional and for a fixed period of time. Policies covering important areas of diocesan life are in effect on an ongoing, longer term basis.

Policies

Canon law (391.2) describes the bishop's executive, judicial, and legislative authority.

The bishop exercises legislative power himself. He exercises executive power either personally or through vicars general or episcopal vicars according to the norm of law. He exercises judicial power either personally or through the judicial vicar and judges according to the norm of law.[7]

General Policies

One way legislative power is exercised is through establishing policies governing important diocesan functions. Table 6.4 shows responses to the survey questions about diocesan-wide policies in five areas. Finances and personnel management are policy areas found in secular organizations

---

7. The Canon Law Society of America, *Code of Canon Law.*

Table 6.4 Diocesan Policies in Different Key Areas of Operation

	No Diocesan Policy (%)	General Guidelines (%)	Specific Guidelines in Key Areas (%)	Detailed, Highly Standardized (%)
Liturgy	4	20	63	13
Sacramental preparation	0	18	65	18
Finances	1	6	44	50
Personnel management	1	15	53	32
Religious education	2	15	65	18

and reflect the bishops' administrative (governance) role. Policies related to liturgy, sacramental preparation, and religious education are specific to religious organizations and emphasize the bishop's sanctifying and teaching roles.

Over 95 percent of bishops reported having at least general guidelines for all five policy areas, and over three-quarters have "specific guidelines in key areas" or "detailed, highly standardized" policies. Half of the bishops reported having detailed financial policies and almost one-third have detailed personnel policies. For the most part, there are no significant differences (based on bishop or diocesan characteristics) in how likely bishops are to have different levels of policy detail. The exception is religious education policies, which the bishops were least likely to report having. Bishops who reported legal issues being a problem were more likely to have more detailed religious education policies. Bishops from the older priest ordination cohorts were more likely than the younger cohorts to have religious education policies.

Safe Environment—Protection of Children and Youth

As discussed in Chapter 5, as of 2016, all of the Latin Rite ordinaries accept the guidelines of the *Charter for the Protection of Children and Young People*.[8]

---

8. United States Conference of Catholic Bishops, *Charter for the Protection of Children and Young People* (Washington, DC, 2018), http://www.usccb.org/issues-and-action/child-and-youth-protection/upload/Charter-for-the-Protection-of-Children-and-Young-People-2018.pdf.

The *Charter* requires dioceses and eparchies to have programs to create and maintain a safe environment, and policies and procedures to respond to allegations of sexual abuse of minors. Based on a review of diocesan websites, every diocese has some information related to safe environment, protection of youth, or sexual abuse reporting/victim assistance. Links to diocesan policy are included on 82 percent of the sites, and codes of conduct or ethics are included on 7 percent. Only 12 percent do not include their safe environment policies on their websites. Although some websites include access to other types of policies, no policy information is as highly visible or consistently available as those related to safe environment and protection of children and youth.

The *Essential Norms for Diocesan/Eparchial Policies Dealing with Allegations of Sexual Abuse of Minors by Priests or Deacons*[9] is a companion document to the *Charter for the Protection of Children and Young People* which requires each diocese to have a written policy on sexual abuse by clergy and other personnel. It includes specific elements that need to be included in these policies. Because of this universal requirement, for all dioceses (presumably 100 percent), policies in this area would be considered "highly detailed and standardized." Only 50 percent of the bishops reported having "highly detailed" finance policies. It may be that the bishops are under-reporting the level of detail of other policy areas, but it is also likely that the safe environment, child protection, and sexual abuse reporting policies are more extensive than other policy areas.

These last two chapters focused on the bishop's governance and administrative roles. The next chapter concentrates on the bishops' teaching and preaching roles.

---

9. United States Conference of Catholic Bishops, *Essential Norms for Diocesan/Eparchial Policies Dealing with Allegations of Sexual Abuse of Minors by Priests or Deacons* (Washington, DC, 2006).

7

The Bishops Speak

If we [bishops] speak out on certain issues, some people will say, "We need a separation of Church and state, and you have no right to comment on that." If we speak out on other issues, another sector of society will say, "We should have a separation of Church and state, and you shouldn't be talking about that." Other times, when we don't speak out, people are saying "Where's the Church? Why aren't you speaking more actively about immigration or healthcare?" Or fill in the blanks with, "Planned Parenthood or contraception or abortion." So there are times when we are told to step back and mind our own business and there are other times that people are looking for the voice of the Church.

BISHOP FROM AN EASTERN DIOCESE

KENNETH WOODWARD, A journalist who covered religion for *Newsweek* from 1964 to 2002, described the kinds of news stories his editors sought:

The editors in the religion department, first of all they wanted stories about Catholics. Second, they wanted stories about Catholics. Third, they wanted stories about Catholics. And fourth, everybody else—until Evangelicals became more politically and publicly active and visible and they wanted stories on them. . . . I remember trying to sell a story about Methodism and I got nowhere. Those are boring people, you see.[1]

---

1. Albert Mohler, "Getting American Religion: A Conversation with Former *Newsweek* Religion Editor Kenneth L. Woodward," December 5, 2016, http://www.albertmohler.com/2016/12/05/getting-american-religion/. Woodward has said this on many occasions. This particular version of the quote has been taken from a very rough interview transcript. We have edited slightly for clarity, punctuation, capitalization, etc.

With this level of interest in Catholicism, it is not surprising that 65 percent of bishops said they have been interviewed on a local secular radio or television channel "often" or "on a regular basis" during the past five years. One bishop said:

> The local media ask to speak with me pretty regularly. In fact, last week I had a flurry of requests because I made a statement about how we should respond to panhandlers in our streets, which is a big local issue right now. But they ask about other issues too, whether it's about abortion, or legalization of marijuana, or driver's licenses for undocumented individuals, or Planned Parenthood—almost any public issue. It's not unusual, at least here in [my diocese], for the secular media to come to the bishop because we are a very Catholic area in terms of percentages.

Our survey results show that bishops do tend to be interviewed somewhat more frequently in dioceses where a relatively high percentage of the population is Catholic. Impressively, however, we find that even in dioceses where Catholics make up a small portion of the population, a majority of bishops still said they have been interviewed "often" or "on a regular basis" during the past five years.[2]

The media attention directed toward the U.S. Catholic Church is probably a mixed blessing for the bishops. When something bad or embarrassing happens in the Church, the Spotlight shined by the press is apt to be glaring. As we saw in Chapter 4, 18 percent of the bishops described "criticism in the secular press or media" as a "great" problem for them, and another 44 percent as "somewhat" of a problem. Nevertheless, most bishops do not shy away from the media. In the survey, 82 percent agreed "strongly" with the statement, "It is important to me to be a spokesman for Catholicism in my diocese." In interviews, many bishops told us that they see interviews with the press as an opportunity to share Catholic positions

---

2. There is a difference between dioceses with lower and higher percentages of Catholics. In dioceses in which Catholics make up less than one-fifth of the population, 57 percent of bishops say they have been interviewed "often" or "on a regular basis" during the past five years. This compares to 82 percent in dioceses in which Catholics make up a fifth or more. Comparing relatively small Catholic populations (e.g., under 10 percent of the surrounding population) and relatively large ones (e.g., over 50 percent of the population) showed similar results.

on public issues or to respond to outside negativity toward the Church. An archbishop summarized this attitude:

> Anytime there is anything controversial in the Church, I am asked by the TV stations to make a statement. They always want an interview. And I never say, "no." . . . Most recently I spoke out about the national election. Of course, I did not speak about the candidates themselves but about the campaigns and about how negative they are. . . . We are teaching our children to grow up with a lack of civility, a lack of respect. . . . Also I certainly spoke out about the religious freedom issue and the HHS mandate from the federal government.[3]

In this chapter we examine two ways bishops speak out publically: teaching the faith to Catholics in their dioceses and asking Catholics to consider the implications of the faith for social issues or politics. We also discuss how bishops feel when they experience resistance from lay Catholics to Church teaching, or criticism in the secular media for the stands they take on issues of the day.

The Bishop as Teacher

The *Catechism of the Catholic Church* emphasizes that a foremost responsibility of the bishops is to teach the Catholic faith to the laity. The role of teaching is closely associated with preaching. Sometimes the two terms are used almost interchangeably:

> Bishops, with priests as co-workers, have as their first task "to preach the Gospel of God to all men," in keeping with the Lord's command. They are "heralds of faith, who draw new disciples to Christ; they are authentic teachers" of the apostolic faith "endowed with the authority of Christ . . . ." The mission of the Magisterium is linked to the definitive nature of the covenant established by God with his people in Christ. It is this Magisterium's task to preserve

---

3. That is, the mandate requiring employers to provide contraception coverage in health insurance plans.

God's people from deviations and defections and to guarantee them the objective possibility of professing the true faith without error.[4]

How important is the role of teaching and upholding tenets of the faith to the U.S. bishops? To answer this question, we asked bishops in the survey the extent to which they agree or disagree with the following statement: "As a bishop I have a special responsibility beyond that of other priests for preserving and upholding the faith." The responses reveal that the role is quite important indeed. A notable 82 percent agreed "strongly," 16 percent agreed "somewhat," 2 percent disagreed "somewhat," and 1 percent disagreed "strongly." Archbishops were more likely than other bishops to agree "strongly" (96 and 78 percent, respectively), perhaps because they are often highly visible public figures. Regardless, teaching is a responsibility that nearly all bishops take quite seriously. Many also enjoy it. A bishop described his experience with teaching in a southern, mostly rural diocese after moving there from a highly Catholic urban area:

> My experience of Catholicism down here is that we're the small puppy. There are a lot of large dogs around the table: you've got the Assemblies of God, fundamentalists, and Pentecostals. We're the little puppy in the corner. But because of that, the Catholics down here are *really* Catholic. They are very proud to be Catholic, and they want to know the teachings of the Church. They're not afraid to live the faith and to profess it. I've been impressed. It's been very edifying to see that. . . . The diocese is [tens of thousands of] square miles, but I don't think of traveling to the parishes and missions as a burden. I think of it as a real opportunity. Whether I'm down in the southwestern part, or up in the northwest, wherever, I'm bringing the Gospel.

Examining open-ended survey responses provided insight on use of the terms *teaching* and *preaching* by the bishops. Recall from Chapter 6 that we asked survey respondents to name the three roles of the bishop that are most important to them personally. How prominent is the teaching role when bishops were not directly prompted about it? Over half (59 percent) of the bishops named teaching as one these roles (or something closely

---

4. *Catechism of the Catholic Church*, no. 888 (New York: Doubleday, 1995).

similar, such as "catechesis" or "guarding integrity of the faith"). An additional 15 percent did not mention teaching but did name "preaching." Thus in total, about three-quarters (74 percent) of bishops gave a response that indicates that teaching and/or preaching is a central role in their lives.

Table 7.1 breaks down the open-ended responses of teaching and preaching by two characteristics: type of bishop and self-described theological orientation. As the first column shows, archbishops were significantly more likely than other bishops to say that teaching is among the roles most important to them (77 compared to 55 percent). Again, it may be that archbishops are especially visible in the public sphere and receive more coverage from the media for their pronouncements. As such, they may feel more acutely that Catholics look to them for guidance.

The second panel in Table 7.1 shows that bishops who described themselves as theologically "traditional" were more likely than both "moderates" and "progressives" to name teaching as an important role (69 percent, compared to 49 and 55 percent respectively). Why might this be? As Hoge and Wenger have argued, traditional or orthodox members of the clergy

Table 7.1 Bishops Naming Teaching or Preaching as Among the Three Most Important Episcopal Roles, by Selected Characteristics

Bishop Characteristic	Teaching[a] (%)	Preaching (But not Teaching) (%)	Either (%)
All	59	15	74
Type of Bishop			
Archbishop	77	14	91
Other ordinary	55	15	70
Self-Described Theological Orientation			
Traditional	69	15	83
Moderate	49	16	65
Progressive	55	15	70

[a] A few respondents named both teaching and preaching as among the most important roles of the bishop. For sake of simplicity, and because it makes the comparisons clearest, we have grouped these individuals under "teaching."

Note: Due to rounding error, numbers in the first two columns may not sum exactly to those in the third.

Source: CARA Survey of Bishops, 2016.

tend to seek and emphasize what is "True."[5] Traditional bishops may place special importance on cultivating adherence to the most basic and long-standing of Catholic doctrines among their flock. They may see the need to stand against encroaching secular thought from general society and creeping relativism within the Church.

Writing Topics

The teaching role of bishops encompasses many things. Among the most fundamental is overseeing Catholic education, which takes place primarily in parishes and Catholic schools. In these settings, Catholics receive instruction on the fundamental doctrines such as the Trinity, the Resurrection, and the Immaculate Conception. But the role of bishops as teachers does not end here. Catholics have more to learn and reflect upon than the basics of their faith, and often bishops take a more direct role in speaking to Catholics about the implications of their faith. Here is how one bishop described what the teaching role means to him:

> The goal is always to take the teachings of Christ and the Church and apply them to the real life circumstances and challenges of the day. That's been the work of the Church for 2,000 years now: to take the Gospel and apply it to the existential circumstances of your own time and place. That happens in lots of different ways. It happens in a formal liturgical way when you are preaching during Mass or at some other public ceremony. It can happen when you do interviews with the media, which is a way of reaching the broader population, especially with the secular media. It can happen if you are writing pastoral letters or letters to your priests or people. In my particular case, it happens in the newspaper articles I write for the diocesan newspaper every two weeks. I have been doing that almost constantly for about twenty-one years now.

In this chapter we are particularly interested in the topics bishops tend to emphasize when they speak directly to Catholics. In crafting a series of

---

5. Dean R. Hoge and Jacqueline E. Wenger, *Evolving Visions of the Priesthood: Changes from Vatican II to the Turn of the New Century* (Collegeville, MN: Liturgical Press, 2003).

items for the questionnaire, we chose to ask bishops specifically about the topics they address when they *write* to Catholics of their dioceses. There are several reasons for this approach. One is that what they say in writing is likely to be carefully thought out. It will not be the kind of extemporaneous remark made in response to a question from an interviewer or a attendee at a "town hall" style meeting. A written letter or column also provides enough space for bishops to really explain why the Church teaches what it does on a particular topic. It is one thing to simply reiterate Catholicism's position on, say, artificial contraception, and quite another to walk someone who is not a theologian through the rather complex and nuanced ideas that undergird this position. Next, a bishop's writing probably reaches more Catholics than his preaching. Not everyone will regularly hear homilies at the cathedral, but the majority of bishops write a column in their diocesan newspaper as way of reaching Catholics throughout their diocese. Of course, interviews in the secular mass media might reach even more people, but also in a more haphazard manner and in a format that allows for selective editing of their remarks. So we asked bishops how frequently they have written on seven general topics in the past five years. Table 7.2 summarizes the responses.

One of the more remarkable results in the table is that, for any given topic, very few bishops said they had "never" written about it in the past five years. The great majority had written on each topic at least "occasionally." This seems to reflect an effort by bishops to speak widely to a variety of important issues and avoid a more narrow focus in their writing. Overall, the topic bishops reported writing on most frequently is Catholic teaching on the sanctity of life, with 38 percent saying they write about it "on a regular basis." This is followed by the rather general topics of "spiritual or biblical reflection" and "Catholic theology" (about one-third each).

Twenty-four percent of bishops reported writing about Catholic social teaching on a regular basis. The relative emphasis on Catholic social teaching versus the sanctity of life will doubtless be of interest to many. Those who see protection of unborn (and other) life as paramount in Catholicism's vision of a good society will surely be heartened that sanctity of life comes out on top in Table 7.2. On the other hand, this result will confirm the beliefs of critics who have felt that the Church's emphasis on abortion comes at the expense of other equally important issues. The next section in this chapter touches on whether and to what extent a tension exists for bishops in addressing these topics.

Archbishops tend to address each of the topics in Table 7.2 somewhat more often than other bishops do. We suspect they may write more often in general. However, the two topics on which archbishops differ

Table 7.2 Topics Bishops Write to Catholics About

"In the last five years, how often have you written to Catholics (e.g., a pastoral letter or column in the diocesan newspaper) on these topics?"

	"Never" (%)	"Occasionally" (%)	"Often" (%)	"On a Regular Basis" (%)
Catholic teaching on sanctity of life	0	18	44	38
Spiritual or biblical reflection	3	27	36	34
Catholic theology	2	33	33	33
Catholic social teaching	0	21	55	24
Catholic teaching on the family	1	22	52	26
Religious freedom issues	4	35	41	23
Catholic teaching on sexual morality	2	51	33	15

Note: The sample for this table excludes a very small number of bishops who responded "never" to all the items (as they presumably do little or no writing).

Due to rounding error, percentages in a row may not sum exactly to 100.

Source: CARA Survey of Bishops, 2016.

most from others are interesting: Catholic teaching on the family, and religious freedom issues. Almost half (48 percent) of archbishops have written about the family on a regular basis, compared to 21 percent of other bishops. Forty-three percent of archbishops have written about religious freedom on a regular basis, compared to 18 percent of other bishops. These differences may reflect controversies that captured national attention in the years prior to our survey. Same-sex marriage was hotly contested in many states (and eventually legalized in more than 30) before being addressed by the Supreme Court in 2015. In 2012 and 2015, several prominent bishops signed ecumenical religious statements in defense of traditional marriage.[6]

---

6. United States Conference of Catholic Bishops, "The Defense of Marriage and Right of Religious Freedom Open Letter 2015," April 23, 2015, http://www.usccb.org/issues-and-action/marriage-and-family/marriage/promotion-and-defense-of-marriage/defense-of-marriage-and-right-of-religious-freedom-open-letter-2015.cfm.

Concern about religious freedom arises from several governmental policies that challenge the conscience of Church institutions. In 2006, Catholic Charities in the Archdioceses of Boston and San Francisco ceased adoption services because of new state policies that would have required the Catholic agencies to possibly place children with same-sex married couples. In 2011, the U.S. Department of Health and Human Service mandated that employers, religious institutions among them, provide employees with health insurance plans covering contraception. Several prominent Catholic archbishops were among those who took the lead to argue that all religious organizations should be exempt from the mandate. In addition to these well-publicized controversies, some bishops expressed general dismay over increasing governmental intrusion into many aspects of Church activities. As we saw in Chapter 4, an archbishop said:

> There has been a desire on the part of government to manage and regulate, not houses of worship so much, but the works that we do that serve the common good, whether it's charities or schools. And there has been a limitation of conscience rights. The most famous, of course, is the HHS mandate. There are also licensure challenges, accreditation challenges, and local ordinances that would take our teaching on marriage and sexuality and frame it up as bigotry and discrimination.

The fact that archbishops have written more often about religious freedom should not be interpreted as meaning that other bishops remain unconcerned about the issue. The survey asked bishops whether they agreed or disagreed with the following statement: "The Catholic Church's right to religious freedom faces increasing threat from the government." An overwhelming 96 percent agreed, with 24 percent agreeing "somewhat" and 72 percent agreeing "strongly." The sense that the Church is under a sort of modern-day persecution seems almost palpable.

Writing Topics and the Church's Unique Social and Cultural Perspective

We wished to understand what factors might lead bishops to write about some issues more frequently than others. Do some bishops prefer to focus their writing on issues that correspond to a "right" perspective or a "left" perspective? Before examining the results of our analyses, it is useful to reflect on Catholicism's rather unique voice in addressing social and political issues.

The Church's stance on the sanctity and protection of life places it on the traditionalist side of issues such as abortion and physician-assisted suicide. Add in U.S. Catholic leaders' advocacy on the issues we have just discussed—traditional marriage and freedom of conscience on contraception—and the Church is aligned with conservatives on society's "cultural" issues. A bishop spoke with us about his pro-life advocacy:

> I communicate the Church's pro-life message mainly through homilies, through my preaching, and through the columns I write for our diocesan newspaper. People often speak to me in positive ways after the Masses I celebrate in parishes. They thank me for speaking so clearly [about abortion]. I also participate in the March for Life that is held every year in [our area]. We have a big Mass. Then we meet at City Hall, have a rally with speeches, and then we march down [the main street of the city] . . . thousands upon thousands of people with our pro-life banners. Many of the parishes from my diocese get involved, which is great. We usually invite speakers from other religions, which is very powerful. It's wonderful to see many other religious groups and denominations participate.

At the same time, the Catholic Church has a history of relatively progressive teachings in the economic realm, which date to the papal encyclical *Rerum Novarum* in 1891 and its emphasis on the rights and dignity of the worker. In the United States, bishops have frequently spoken out for assistance to the poor and needy. For example, the 2002 pastoral on poverty, *A Place at the Table*, reaffirmed Catholic support for living wages, universal access to health care, and debt reduction for developing nations.[7] In recent years, the bishops have increasingly spotlighted the plight of immigrants as well. The 2000 pastoral *Welcoming the Stranger Among Us* advocated legalization opportunities for undocumented immigrants and

---

7. United States Conference of Catholic Bishops, *A Place at the Table: A Catholic Recommitment to Overcome Poverty and to Respect the Dignity of all God's Children*, November 13, 2002, http://www.usccb.org/issues-and-action/human-life-and-dignity/poverty/place-at-the-table.cfm.

improved treatment of refugees.[8] A bishop described to us how he has recently spoken out on this topic:

> [This diocese] is greatly impacted by environmental concerns. . . .
> I wrote an op-ed piece for our local newspaper that the paper very
> happily printed in its entirety. Basically, the position of my piece was
> that we have a moral responsibility to assist climate change refugees. A few days later the paper had an opinion poll and it asked,
> "Do you agree with Bishop _____ that we have a moral obligation to
> assist climate change refugees?" And I think about sixty percent of
> the people said "no" and about thirty percent said "yes."

Returning to the writing topics, 24 percent of bishops said they write about the sanctity of life more frequently than Catholic social teaching. Conversely, 9 percent write about Catholic social teaching more frequently than the sanctity of life [these percentages are not shown in Table 7.2 but rather come from a cross-tabulation of the two items]. Not surprisingly, the theological orientation of the bishops contributes to this. Among self-described traditional bishops, 35 percent write about the sanctity of life more frequently than Catholic social teaching; and 4 percent write about Catholic social teaching more frequently. In contrast, among progressive bishops, 20 percent write about the sanctity of life more frequently and 35 percent write about Catholic social teaching more frequently.

Still, it's useful to keep in mind that roughly two-thirds of all bishops (66 percent) reported writing about the two topics with equal frequency. Some bishops we spoke with in interviews—rather than seeing a them as being at odds—readily embraced what an outside observer might view as an inherent tension between the Church's "right" and "left" positions.

A bishop who speaks forcefully on both types of issues described his philosophy:

> If there's one word or phrase that summarizes my approach to teaching
> as a bishop, it's the sense of having a prophetic voice. . . . Now some
> people call it being a "culture warrior." Alright, that's fine, whatever
> term they want to use. I prefer to call it being a prophet, because
> that's what prophets do. They take the word of God and they apply

---

8. United States Conference of Catholic Bishops, *Welcoming the Stranger Among Us: Unity in Diversity*, November 15, 2000, http://www.usccb.org/issues-and-action/cultural-diversity/pastoral-care-of-migrants-refugees-and-travelers/resources/welcoming-the-stranger-among-us-unity-in-diversity.cfm.

it to current, contemporary circumstances. I think the Church has a very important role to play in that regard. . . . Sometimes when we speak out on issues we are accused of being too liberal, and some-times when we speak out on issues we are accused of being too con-servative. But that just is the nature of the prophetic voice, I think. We try to address these issues as faithfully as we can.

Another bishop said he encourages lay Catholics to turn away from a "conventional" left–right way of thinking about issues. His diocese has many Hispanic Catholics, and he described to us how he asks the laity to see abor-tion and immigration as deeply interconnected rather than disparate issues:

Our folks here [lay people] who are against abortion tend to be more anti-abortion than pro-life, quite honestly. . . . Folks against abortion have been folks who are also anti-immigrant. What we learned in out-reach to pregnant women [in my former diocese] is that women can often face emergency pregnancies alone and abandoned. . . . But here it is very different. Hispanic families are very robust, and even if the woman feels shame, she generally has support from her extended family. So I have an op-ed piece this weekend explaining that if you want to save the unborn you have to walk with the undocumented because the family members who are assisting pregnant women are in a variety of places with regard to their legal status. Their experience of racism and anti-immigrant attitudes, the criminalization of eleven million undocu-mented, the unending fear of deportation—it's not the environment we need in order to reach out to families in these situations. And this is very counter-intuitive to the national narrative. If you want to reach the un-born, you have to love the undocumented and you have to respect them. You have to care for them and support them. A few folks don't like those issues merged together, but it has helped me clarify for folks that, yes, abortion is an anchor issue for all other issues of life and justice.

Besides a bishop's theological orientation, what might affect the types of topics he writes about? One possible factor we wished to examine is the local political context. By political context we mean whether a diocese is located in an area that is generally Republican, generally Democrat, or politically mixed. We analyzed this at the state level, which is imprecise be-cause most dioceses are smaller than the states that contain them (but this approach is considerably simpler than trying to code the dioceses them-selves). We categorized states as "red, blue, and purple" based on results of the three previous presidential elections.[9] White Catholics tend to be a little more conservative in areas of the country where the rest of the population is generally conservative—and a little more liberal in areas that are generally liberal.[10] Is there any tendency for bishops to "play to their audience," so to speak? We found no evidence of this. The frequency with which bishops write about topics such as the sanctity of life or Catholic social teaching does not vary by whether they reside in a blue or red state.

Applying the Faith to Social Issues and Politics

Catholic leaders, from parish priests to the pope, are bombarded with opinions on whether they should or should not speak out on issues of the day—and if so, on which particular issues. When the U.S. bishops published *Economic Justice for All* in 1986,[11] some thinkers on the right urged them to leave economics to the economists and focus on the purely "religious" realm. Conservative Catholic James Kilpatrick said, derisively:

> The bishops know the workings of the marketplace by hearsay; they themselves, living well-fed and protected lives, are as innocent as kittens of economic risk and insecurity. When they involve the church in lobbying for changes at the World Bank and the IMF, all in the name of moral instruction, they trespass on the boundary that wisely separates the pulpit from the political arena.[12]

On economic matters the left has been perhaps equally vociferous in its critiques of the bishops, except the problem in this case is that Church's leaders have remained too silent. In advance of a 2013 assembly of the

---

9. We coded states as purple if, in any of the three prior presidential elections (2004, 2008, and 2012), votes for the Democrat and Republican candidates were within five percentage points of each other. We excluded the Archdiocese for the Military and the Diocese of St. Thomas in the Virgin Islands from analyses.

10. Pew Research Center Forum on Religion & Public Life, "The Catholic 'Swing' Vote," October 11, 2012, http://www.pewforum.org/2012/10/11/the-catholic-swing-vote/.

11. United States Conference of Catholic Bishops, *Economic Justice for All: Pastoral Letter on Catholic Social Teaching and the U.S. Economy* (1986).

12. James Kilpatrick, "Bishops Could Take a Tip from Burke," *Detroit Free Press*, November 20, 1986, 9.

USCCB in Baltimore, two liberal Catholic groups called on its attendees to speak out more on issues of poverty.[13] They urged:

> Since the global economy was brought to the edge of collapse by the sub-prime mortgage scandal, the USCCB has failed to collectively and effectively address poverty—even once. . . . There has been a growing school of thought that percolates among some bishops and beyond their circles—and sometimes into the public square—that the US bishops should not involve themselves in economic affairs because you are not economists. Such a perspective surrenders moral imperatives that can shape economic policy and creates an *advocacy gap* that has diminished the effectiveness of the US bishops' prophetic voice as paracletes for the poor.[14]

As a bishop wryly observed in the quote that opens this chapter, whether one believes religious leaders should speak out on politics seems to depend less on one's philosophy regarding church and state than on the particular issue at hand.

We were interested in the extent to which individual bishops step across the invisible line some people perceive (when it suits them perhaps) as separating the spiritual and temporal realms. How often do the bishops call for reflection or action regarding politics or vital issues of the day? We asked survey respondents four questions on this topic. Table 7.3 summarizes the results.

We were particularly interested in how bishops speak out in the context of elections. The criticism they receive for lack of balance or overstepping their bounds often arises as elections approach.[15] Many bishops reported that they have asked Catholics to consider Catholic teaching when voting for candidates, with 38 percent saying they have done so "on a regular

13. Joshua J. McElwee, "Groups Urge US Bishops to Speak on Poverty, Build 'Church for the Poor,'" *National Catholic Reporter*, November 11, 2013, https://www.ncronline.org/blogs/ncr-today/groups-urge-us-bishops-speak-poverty-build-church-poor.

14. Catholic Democrats and Catholics in Alliance for the Common Good, 2013. Untitled letter to the candidates for president of the US Conference of Catholic Bishops (USCCB). Available at http://catholicdemocrats.org/BishopLetter.pdf.

15. See, for example, Tom Roberts, "At USCCB Meeting, Bishops Slow to Adopt Pope's Vision," *National Catholic Reporter*, December 1, 2015, https://www.ncronline.org/news/vatican/parsing-priorities-and-plans-meeting-bishops-slow-adopt-popes-vision.

Table 7.3 Issues Where Bishops Engage in Political or Policy Activity

"In the last five years, how often have you . . .?"	"Never" (%)	"Occasionally" (%)	"Often" (%)	"On a Regular Basis" (%)
Asked Catholics to consider Catholic teaching when voting for candidates	8	18	37	38
Lobbied lawmakers or other political leaders about law or policy	4	28	43	24
Made statements to the general public about current social or political issues	7	26	47	21
Asked Catholics to vote a particular way on a ballot initiative or referendum	49	38	13	1

Note: Due to rounding, percentages in a row may not sum exactly to 100.

Source: CARA Survey of Bishops, 2016.

basis" during the past five years and 37 percent that they have done so "often." A bishop said:

> I do not tell Catholics [in my diocese] to vote for a specific candidate. What I do tell them is not to vote for someone who opposes our values. I tell them to make sure that the candidate they choose conforms to Catholic teaching. I make every effort not to be seen as "pro" any party, but that doesn't mean that I don't teach clearly about the issues.

A majority of bishops have lobbied political leaders at least "often," and a majority also made statements to the general public about current social or political issues. The frequency with which bishops have spoken out varies little by self-described theological orientation. In other words, conservative and liberal bishops gave fairly similar answers in response to these items. It seems clear that most bishops see an important role for the Church and its teachings in guiding political thought and action.

Much less common among the bishops is asking Catholics to vote a particular way on a ballot initiative or referendum. This may reflect the reality that such ballot measures vary widely from state to state. In some states they are rare to nonexistent or consist largely of symbolic statements on relatively mundane issues. In other states, ballot initiatives are an important part of the lawmaking process and have addressed highly contentious issues. For example, in 2012, bishops in Maine, Maryland, Minnesota, and Washington state condemned various ballot items to legalize same-sex marriage in those states.[16] In the same year, Massachusetts bishops spoke against an initiative that would allow doctors to prescribe suicide drugs to terminally ill patients.[17]

In contrast to the topics on which bishops write, archbishops tend not to stand out with regard to the items in Table 7.3. In general, they reported speaking out about as frequently as other bishops about elections and political issues. Neither are there notable differences based on the bishops' theological orientation; self-described conservatives speak out roughly as often as self-described progressives. Yet, we did uncover an interesting difference among bishops based on whether their dioceses are located in red or blue states. Bishops in red states have most frequently asked Catholics to consider Catholic teaching when voting for candidates. Almost half (48 percent) reported having done so "on a regular basis" during the last five years. This compares to 36 percent of bishops in purple states and 26 percent in blue states. Perhaps bishops are more likely to perceive the laity as receptive to messages about Catholic teaching and voting where Catholics (and the electorate generally) are relatively more conservative. However, this does not seem to extend to the other ways of speaking out listed in Table 7.3, such as lobbying lawmakers or making statements to the general public.

---

16. Patricia Zapor, "Voters in Three States Approve Laws Permitting Same-Sex Marriage," November 9, 2012, *Catholic News Service*, http://www.catholicnews.com/services/englishnews/2012/voters-in-three-states-approve-laws-permitting-same-sex-marriage-cns-1204732.cfm.

17. Sarah Favot, "Lowell-area Catholics Hear Bishop Decry Assisted Suicide," *Lowell Sun*, February 13, 2012.

Richard Ducket, "Bishop Attacks Question 2; Ballot Initiative 'Morally Flawed,'" *Sunday Telegram* (Massachusetts), October 28, 2012, B1.

The Clergy Sexual Abuse Scandal and the Church's Perceived Credibility

There were many aspects to the shock, dismay, and anger lay Catholics experienced in 2002 during the large-scale national revelations of clergy sexual abuse within the Church. Foremost among them were sympathy for the victims, disbelief about the magnitude of the problem, and outrage about cases where superiors were inadequate in addressing the problem. In this section we wish to examine another concern that has arisen in the wake of these revelations—that the scandal has hampered Church leaders in other ways, particularly their ability to speak with credibility and authority. In the wake of the scandals in 2002, Francis Fiorenza, a Catholic studies professor at Harvard Divinity School, said, "One of the major tragedies of the recent scandals has been precisely the loss of moral authority at a time when such moral authority is most needed."[18]

Are people now disregarding what the bishops have to say on issues of the day? Certainly one can find anecdotes to this effect. Writing in the *New Yorker* about a capital murder case in Louisiana, reporter Rachel Aviv relates prosecutor Dale Cox's rejection of the Church's position on the death penalty. Among other factors, Cox mentioned the sexual abuse issue as a reason for discounting this teaching:

> Cox, who is Catholic and went to a Jesuit school, was opposed to the death penalty at the start of his career, and in 1983, after working in the district attorney's office for six years, he left, because he didn't feel comfortable pursuing capital cases. He believed that it was God's decision when to end someone's life. He joined a civil firm while working part time as a special prosecutor. By 2011, when he returned to the office full time, he said that his thinking had evolved. After constant exposure to violence, he began to reinterpret the Bible. He thought about passages in which Christ was judgmental and unforgiving—Christ's belief that it would be better if Judas Iscariot had never been born, for instance—and saw Him as retaliatory in ways that he hadn't appreciated before. After the

---

18. Patricia Rice, "Catholics Hope Policy Will Revive Church's Moral Clout," *St. Louis Post-Dispatch*, November 24, 2002, B1.

Church's pedophilia scandals, Cox no longer felt obliged to follow its teachings precisely.[19]

In the survey we asked bishops to agree or disagree with the following statement: "Media coverage of clergy sexual abuse has made it challenging to present or defend Church teachings in my diocese." A majority agreed, with 43 percent agreeing "somewhat" and 20 percent agreeing "strongly." Thirty percent disagreed "somewhat," and just 8 percent disagreed "strongly." Table 7.4 shows the relationship between these responses and several other factors. There is no significant difference between archbishops and other ordinaries. And, somewhat surprisingly, the results show no relationship with the ministry of bishops in 2002. Those who were already bishops in their current dioceses do not significantly differ from those who were bishops in other dioceses or who were still priests in other dioceses.[20] We had expected that those who were already bishops at the time of the scandal, especially in their current diocese, would be fighting a stronger headwind in this regard.

Instead, what seems most important is the region of the country where a bishop's current diocese is located. Bishops in the Northeast were significantly more likely than those in other regions to agree "strongly" that it is challenging to present or defend Church teaching due to the scandal. This finding seems consistent with CARA polls of lay Catholics taken during 2002. Catholics in the Northeast region expressed considerably more awareness and anger regarding the scandal than Catholics elsewhere. Some of this may be proximity to Boston and greater exposure to news from that archdiocese. Further, we suspect that secular news media in other cities in New England were particularly aggressive in their reporting of the scandal so as not to be shown up by the *Boston Globe*. Indeed, the final panel in Table 7.4 shows a correlation between difficulty defending Church teaching and the amount of media coverage bishops said has been directed at the scandal in their diocese. We asked a bishop in the Northeast

---

19. Rachel Aviv, "Revenge Killing: Race and the Death Penalty in a Louisiana Parish," *The New Yorker*, July 6 and 13, 2015, http://www.newyorker.com/magazine/2015/07/06/revenge-killing.

20. There are very few bishops in our sample who were priests in their current diocese in 2002—too few for meaningful analysis.

Table 7.4 Response to Media Coverage of Clergy Sex Abuse Scandal by Selected Characteristics

"Media coverage of clergy sexual abuse has made it challenging to present or defend Church teaching in my diocese"

Bishop Characteristic	"Disagree Strongly or Somewhat" (%)	"Agree Somewhat" (%)	"Agree Strongly" (%)
All	38	43	20
Type of Bishop			
Archbishop	38	42	21
Other ordinary	36	42	22
Ministry in 2002			
Priest in another diocese	36	43	21
Bishop in another diocese	41	41	17
Bishop in current diocese	28	50	22
Major Census Region			
Midwest	43	49	9
South	44	42	15
West	33	41	26
Northeast	14	36	50
Media coverage of clergy sexual abuse in the diocese			
"Little or no" or "some" coverage	47	39	14
"A large amount" of coverage	26	41	33
"Extensive" coverage	18	46	36

Note: Due to rounding, percentages in a row may not sum exactly to 100.

Source: CARA Survey of Bishops, 2016.

if he still heard negative comments from laity in his diocese about the scandal:

> We do get comments, and sometimes people use it as a club to beat you over the head about any issue you talk about. Whether it's care for the poor, immigration, or whatever the issue, there will be some people who will throw that back at you and say, "You know what? You should take care of your own [abusive] priests."

Criticism and Pushback from Laity and the Media

In this final section we share stories and reflections of several bishops on criticism or resistance they have received for their positions. Of course, criticism from lay Catholics is not uncommon in the life of a bishop. One told us that preaching at Mass is the only thing he is not criticized for. However, when controversial issues are at play, tempers can run particularly high. In personal interviews, we asked bishops if they ever experienced negativity from laity due to stances taken by themselves as individuals or the bishops collectively. Most could readily recall being on the receiving end of anger. A bishop described such an instance to us:

> Just prior to the invasion of Iraq, I issued a pastoral letter saying that as far as I could judge, the war was going to be unjust and therefore participation in it was going to be immoral. . . . My letter was pretty positively received by priests of the diocese. But there was one parish with a lot of police and ex-military parishioners. The pastor there instructed everyone to read the letter without comment [during a Mass], and it was a fairly lengthy letter. He said it turned into a reaction like the prime minister in Parliament: boos and heckling. [After that] I got a few irate letters.

Another bishop talked with us about reactions to the Church's opposition toward efforts to legalize same-sex marriage in his state:

> Same-sex marriage has been quite the hot button issue [in my diocese]. Most people know where the Church stands. Of course, I have gotten some negative correspondence from people who disagree with our stance. Where I get the most questions about this is from kids at schools, usually from non-Catholic kids who attend our Catholic grammar schools. I do my best to articulate our teaching in a way that they can understand. . . . Most of the drama around this issue occurred here before I was named as bishop here. My predecessor had to deal with the state [debate] on same-sex marriage. He took the brunt of the heat that the media and the general public directed toward the Church. It was truly sad and actually frightening to learn of the vehemence directed toward him; he even received death threats. Some horrible graffiti was scrawled on the walls of the cathedral and the chancery office.

One bishop we interviewed told us he tries to avoid speaking about politics or political issues because of the conflict it can cause with laity. Most bishops, however, are more apt to speak their minds and then take a respectful and pastoral approach with those who disagree. One says:

> There is some negativity with [the Church's stand on] cultural issues. If you are not with the crowd [on these issues], you are accused of being "judgmental" with folks. That's a reason for what Pope Francis is trying to model for bishops and priests. If you are accompanying your people, then difficult situations are not as negative because the people understand the teachings of the Church in the light of the Gospel.

Another bishop also emphasizes the importance of respectful engagement with those who take exception to the Church's positions:

> I just had a letter from somebody that didn't like our, the bishops', statement on immigration. This is the second time somebody wrote me a letter about that. I wrote back and said, "Number one, I'm thrilled you read the statement." [Laughs]. I said that my grandma's name was Loretta Catherine _____ [an obviously Irish surname]. She used to work for German Protestants, and they wouldn't hire the Irish. This was in the days before Social Security . . . I'm talking about 1910: "Irish need not apply." She changed her name to Gertrude because it was more conducive [to being hired]. Loretta Catherine was too Irish, too Catholic. I said, "What would this policy have done to her?" And plus, you have to wrestle with: "I was a stranger and you welcomed me." So, anyway, negative things do come across my desk. . . . But I try to put a positive spin on it, and I try not to take it as a personal attack on me. I try not to get flustered.

Experiences of negativity from the secular media are not as universal among the bishops as are those from lay Catholics—at least when it comes to negativity directed at them personally rather than the Church or its leadership generally. From interviews, much seems to depend on whether the local press takes an aggressive stance when reporting on diocesan matters. One factor raised by several bishops we spoke with is whether a diocese is located in an area where people are relatively religious or relatively secular.

Bishops tend to perceive the press as being more hostile to Catholicism in secularized areas. For example, we asked a bishop in a southern and very religious state whether criticism in the secular media has been a problem for him. He replied:

> Nationally, yes [media negativity is a problem]. Locally, no, because I try to foster relationships with the local media. I've taken the editor-in-chief of the local newspaper out to lunch. . . . And I try as much as possible to be very upfront with the press. When we do anything, we issue a press release. For example, a few years ago the economy here was really struggling. Over a million dollars of our operating budget dried up. So that necessitated layoffs in our pastoral staff. . . . Companies in the area were laying off too, but we knew that ours would be of particular interest [to the media]. We created a press release for the local newspaper, and I was available for questions, as was our chancellor. They got the press release, and they called the chancellor and got all their questions answered. There was a front-page story in the local newspaper, but at least it was our story. We sent them all the information.

We spoke with a bishop in a relatively secularized and urban area. He has often spoken publically with compassion about immigrants and the poor in our society, in addition to advocating a pro-life position on abortion and the traditional model of marriage. Local newspapers frequently label him a "conservative" or even "ultraconservative" bishop.[21] If not unfair, this designation certainly lacks nuance. He described to us the hostility toward Catholicism in the local press, especially toward its traditional moral teachings:

> I find there is truly an inherent bias in the secular media against Catholics, especially in this area. It is something you see all the time. . . . There have been letters to the editor in the local newspapers opposing the Church's teaching. . . . I have offered op-ed pieces on a few occasions to the main local newspaper but they have never published them. What I have found is that they usually publish just one side, the side that they favor. There has not been

---

21. If you begin to type his name [we will call him Bishop John Cerva] into the google search box, the first suggestion it brings up is "Bishop John Cerva conservative."

too much directed against me personally [in the media], but I did have one particular instance of a direct attack against me when I had to intervene in an issue concerning the contracts of teachers in our Catholic schools. We were trying to make sure that they upheld Catholic morality not just in the classroom but also in their personal lives. Given the very secular nature of our area, this was a big news item for a while. . . . I was told that I was interfering in other people's private lives and that that was wrong. The way I saw it, it was just like people getting fired from their jobs for their personal positions on social issues, like the case of the owner of a professional basketball team who was fired for the racist comments he made. . . . He got fired for the awful comments he made using his own private phone and doing so on his own time, not company time. If a basketball team can have a moral philosophy, a moral position, why can't the Church, which represents the teaching of Jesus Christ, have one?

The same bishop continued, discussing ways that media negativity toward the Church has permeated other areas of his ministry, including issues that are not overtly political:

Over the past year [2016–2017] whenever a black person was killed by a white police officer, even if it happened in a totally different part of the country, we would have demonstrations in the city. So they [local newspapers and television] would ask me to comment on that situation. Thankfully, in those cases, I have found the media to be fair and accurate. We did have one case, however, when they were not fair at all. A grandmother tried to blackmail us. She had a grandchild with special needs who was preparing for First Communion. The religious education teachers said that the child was not ready to receive due to the fact that he kept spitting out the practice host that they used to prepare the children to receive Holy Communion. The woman said to us: "If you don't give my grandchild First Communion, I will go to the press." Well, she was on the evening news that very day. There was no offer to allow us to explain our side. The slant was so negative that I had a few angry nuns come up to me at an event shortly thereafter to give me a piece of their mind. I said, "Sisters, would you like to hear the other side of the story?" Once they heard it, they realized that we had made the right decision.

We turned to the survey data to test whether or not media criticism is indeed a systematically greater problem for bishops in more secular areas. As we have seen, 44 percent of all the bishops said criticism in the secular press or media is "somewhat" of a problem for them, and another 18 percent said it is "a great" problem. Table 7.5 shows how these responses vary by several factors. Under the heading "Religiosity of State,"

Table 7.5 Criticism in Secular Press or Media by Selected Characteristics

"How much of a problem is 'criticism in the secular press or media' on a day-to-day basis?"

Bishop Characteristic	"No or Very Little Problem" (%)	"Somewhat of a Problem" (%)	"A Great Problem" (%)
All	38	44	18
Type of bishop			
Archbishop	38	33	29
Other ordinary	37	48	16
Theological orientation			
Traditional	41	29	29
Moderate	28	58	14
Progressive	43	52	5
Religiosity of State			
Relatively religious	50	33	17
Average	43	43	15
Relatively secular	19	57	24
Media coverage of clergy sexual abuse in the diocese			
"Little or no" or "some" coverage	45	45	10
"A large amount" of coverage	30	41	30
"Extensive" coverage	27	45	27

Note: Due to rounding, percentages in a row may not sum exactly to 100.

Source: CARA Survey of Bishops, 2016.

we created three categories based on the religious commitment of people in the states where dioceses are located.[22] Results show little difference between relatively religious and secular states in the likelihood that bishops said criticism is a "great" problem. However, there is a statistically significant difference in whether or not they said it is at least "somewhat" of a problem (50 percent of bishops in religious states, compared to 81 percent in secular states). Thus, it seems plausible that the media is indeed more hostile toward bishops in more secularized dioceses.

Among other notable findings in Table 7.5, self-described traditional bishops are significantly more likely than progressive bishops to describe criticism in the press as "a great problem" (29 compared to 5 percent). Is this an issue of perception by the bishops themselves? It seems possible that traditional bishops genuinely receive more criticism to the extent that they become identified with the Church's teachings on cultural issues such as abortion, homosexuality, and contraception. Not surprisingly, bishops were also significantly more likely to say that criticism in the secular press or media is a great problem for them if the sexual abuse issue received relatively more media coverage in their dioceses.[23]

To summarize this chapter, when the bishops speak out on issues of the day, they do so in their capacity as teachers of the faith. This is one of the three central roles identified for bishops in the *Catechism*; survey responses suggest the role is important to them and that they take it seriously. A typical bishop writes often to Catholics in his diocese on a variety of topics. Among topics we examined, sanctity of life is the one most frequently addressed in bishops' writings, but a majority of bishops also write frequently about Catholic social teaching. Most bishops perceive the Church's right of religious freedom to be under threat from the government; while most have written often about this topic in recent years, archbishops have done so with particular frequency.

Almost three-quarters of bishops say they often or regularly asked Catholics to consider Catholic teaching when voting for candidates.

---

22. We used results from a 2014 survey by the Pew Research Center called the Religious Landscape Study. Pew researchers created an index of the religiosity of states based on the responses of people residing there. Using this index, we coded states as follows: below 50 = "secular"; 50–59 = "average"; 60 and above = "religious." Michael Lipka and Benjamin Wormald, "How Religious is Your State?" Pew Research Center, February 29, 2016, http://www.pewresearch.org/fact-tank/2016/02/29/how-religious-is-your-state/.

23. Note that the differences between archbishops and bishops in Table 7.5 are not statistically significant.

Bishops in red states are more likely to have done so regularly. Additionally most bishops have often or regularly spoken to the general public about issues of the day.

A majority of bishops agree that the clergy sexual abuse scandal has made it challenging to present or defend Church teachings in their diocese. This is particularly true for those who reside in the Northeast or in a diocese where the scandal has received a considerable amount of coverage in the media.

About six in ten bishops say that criticism in the secular press or media is at least "somewhat" of a problem for them. The proportion is higher for those who live in relatively secular states and lower for those who live relatively religious states. Bishops who describe themselves as theologically traditional are considerably more likely than progressives to describe such criticism as a "great" problem.

The final section of this book invites a different kind of criticism, so to speak. We have asked several people with lifelong experience working in the U.S. Church to read what we have written and share their reactions, reflections, and considerable wisdom.

Commentaries

Helen Alvaré

If you take seriously, as I do, the notions of apostolic succession and the necessity of the Church manifesting "God with us" today, alive in the world, then this account of the U.S. bishops provides wonderful food for thought.

It provides cause for grounded hope. These are good men with strong habits of sacrifice, prayer, and service, while living in a "me-first" society. In fact, one of the most uplifting—and yes, surprising—aspects of the entire survey was the amount of time the vast majority of bishops spend praying. Having sat in on countless meetings with bishops wielding calendars bleeding blue ink (into two or three years hence), I was frankly surprised at this good news. But only a tad less surprised than when I learned how many of them exercise regularly. I would imagine it's a matter of absolute necessity, again, given what I have experienced of their insane schedules.

Likewise their simple goodness was revealed in their moving accounts about deriving solid hope from encounters with young Catholics and with their seminarians and priests. Given their duties, I could never imagine how a bishop could go on without these sensibilities, and so I am quite relieved to learn that they exist.

At the same time, I was disappointed to see so little mention of or *collaboration* with women, including women religious, though a majority stated

Professor Helen Alvaré is a Professor of Law at Antonin Scalia Law School, George Mason University. She is a consultor for the Pontifical Council of the Laity (Vatican City), an advisor to the U.S. Conference of Catholic Bishops, founder of WomenSpeakforThemselves.com, and an ABC news consultant. She cooperates with the Permanent Observer Mission of the Holy See to the United Nations as a speaker and a delegate to various United Nations conferences concerning women and the family.

that women should have more leadership roles in parishes and dioceses. There was some, but too little advocacy for collaboration, considering especially women's very high level of activity in the faith, and how far the contemporary world has moved to include women's gifts in every aspect of society. This helped me to understand why—though it easily could—the bishops' together have failed to forward a "women's agenda" comprised of many of their wonderful policies which do *already* disproportionately benefit women. It helped me to understand why they are not making the best "women's case" on neuralgic subjects like contraception, sex, and marriage; though I do believe they are doing an excellent job making that case on abortion. But overall regarding women, they are leaving 20-dollar bills on the ground in my view—leaving themselves on the defensive when they rather have a positive case to make.

The data confirmed a long-held suspicion I have that most bishops are not driven importantly by a desire to influence public policy. They genuinely love teaching and catechesis, scripture and sacraments. This seems as it should be! But it also explains accusations one hears from time to time that the national bishops' conference is the tail wagging the dog. A building of strong public policy experts will naturally have different day-to-day priorities than a body of bishops. When the bishops surveyed did say favorable things about the national Conference, however, they praised work connected to their pastoral priorities; they praised the quality of the USCCB's orientation for international priests, the sexual abuse norms, and the lay ecclesial ministry norms. Several expressed doubts, on the other hand, about the efficacy of the USCCB's various public policy statements.

Given so many bishops' lack of strong attraction for public policy, I was quite surprised to see the amount of time they spend reading and listening to news. I have no idea about the causes of this choice. Is it the wide variety of people with whom they must regularly converse? The possibility that they will be asked to speak publicly on a diverse array of subjects? Whatever the answer, it is my humble opinion that these men who work so much harder than the average U.S. male, might reclaim some of their valuable time by spending less of it on news, the vast majority of which seems repetitive and shallow to me.

Continuing with the subject of bishops' work ethic, it seems to me that they deserve a round of applause from time to time for having to master such a diverse array of competencies: administration, teaching, finance, personnel, sanctification, to name the leading categories. It is rare to find management talent of this level in commerce or government. It should be applauded in the Catholic Church, given how often such talent is displayed. At the same time, because not all bishops have an equal level of talent in all areas, I have always wondered why there are not more auxiliary bishops. This survey kept the question alive in my mind.

It was simply delightful to read about a group of men above politics in this age. This was true of the bishops when I lobbied and spoke on their behalf, and it remains true today. It puts them in creative tension with government at every level, with the media, and even with their own people. Of course, I think that their views falling on the "left" of the political continuum are what people hope most will emerge from the Democrats; and their views on the "right" are what people hope most will emerge from the Republicans. In my view, therefore, they are desperately needed in the public square today precisely to explain in contemporary and common-good terms, where we stand and why. The survey makes it clear how highly educated and competent they are. They need to devote some of this considerable brain power to how to communicate often nuanced positions to the wider society. And not just to help "the flock."

Perhaps I am reflecting my perch at a state university, but I think there would be more and better reception than the bishops currently imagine of straight talk about what love, freedom, and equality *really* require in contemporary U.S. society. And not just because the public retains some fascination with Catholics and our ancient ways. But also because our ideas rest on both reason and love. Yes, resistance to our participation is rife. As one bishop noted, it's ridiculous that a basketball team can sometimes more easily broadcast its moral stance than a bishop! As a lifetime practitioner of "giving a reason for the hope that is in you" where Church meets world, however, I can assure the bishops that—with time devoted to tone, research, and phrasing—they would only be too welcome and too needed in the public square.

Sharon Euart, RSM

Recently, one of my millennial nieces asked me "What does a bishop do all day?" The question gave me pause and then, my 14 years working with

Sister Sharon Euart is a Religious Sister of Mercy who holds a doctorate in canon law. She is the Executive Director of the Resource Center for Religious Institutes. Prior to coming to RCRI, she was the Executive Coordinator of the Canon Law Society of America. She has been a canonical consultant for religious institutes and diocesan bishops. She also has been Associate General Secretary to the United States Conference of Catholic Bishops.

bishops at the USCCB, followed by even more time as a canon law consultant, flashed through my mind. The new CARA survey of U.S. Bishops provides a snapshot of a bishop's profile and even permits a glimpse of his day. The book compiles an enormous amount of data about bishops' lives, ministries, work ethic, prayer life, challenges, hopes, joys; their relationship with other bishops, priests, religious and laity; and their writings and contacts with media. This information and analysis is thought provoking—especially because of a heightened awareness of the complexity of a bishop's life and a new appreciation for the multiple roles a bishop fills in serving his local church.

In examining the governing role of bishops, for example, the survey focuses on the challenges related to the staffing of parishes in a time of fewer priests for active ministry: a mere 14 percent of the bishops responded that the challenge was "little" or "no" problem. At the same time, objective observers, including some bishops, realize that some parishes that were founded and flourished in times past, often to serve immigrant populations, are no longer needed. Over the years, several options or strategies, some more effective and efficient than others, have been adopted to address the reality of a dearth of ordained priests for parish ministry and the changing times. Depending on the local circumstances as well as the decisions of bishops, these options for restructuring have met with more or less success; some options have been modified after the appointment of a new diocesan bishop; and still others have remained untried.

The one-priest pastor for multiple parishes is the option most frequently implemented by the bishops, second only to promoting an increase in vocations. This model can be difficult for the priest, if he is expected to function as an effective pastor capable of shepherding all parishes entrusted to him, rather than as a coordinator of pastoral ministry for some. Though this model can be implemented somewhat quickly, it is important that its impact—that is, the benefits and the limitations of the structure on the priests and the people—be carefully considered. In looking to the future, it is encouraging that only a 5 percent increase is anticipated in bishops either "willing" or "very willing" to utilize this strategy.

In *Evangelii gaudium* Pope Francis describes the parish as

not an outdated institution; precisely because it possesses great flexibility, it can assume quite different contours depending on the openness and missionary creativity of the pastor of the community. . . . We must admit, though, that the call to review and renew our parishes has not yet sufficed to bring them nearer to people, to make them environments of living communion and participation, and to make them completely mission-oriented.[1]

Reflecting Pope Francis, the CARA report indicates that current planning for restructuring parishes is more "pastorally focused" and that processes for assessing parish configurations must be more mission-oriented and related more closely to "broader areas of diocesan leadership."

These data also relate to the survey's findings on collaboration and consultation. In the report on the bishops' relationship with church personnel, the data describe a "complex relationship" with priests, ranging from a problem with a priest and the decreasing number of priests available for ministry, to a sense of being accepted by his priests and the experience of criticism from priests. The data suggest that the challenges inherent in the dual relationship of a bishop to his priests—"brother" and "leader/employer"—add to the complexity and the tension of the bishops' experience with their priests as their "chief collaborators." Nonetheless, the data and the bishops' interviews suggest that the bishops are aware of the potential for tension and seek new ways to develop healthy and effective relationships with their priests.

The survey reports that working with women and men religious ranked low among the problem areas facing bishops, yet 20 percent of the bishops reported having "somewhat" or "a great" problem with women religious. The analysis does not indicate what the problem areas might be; however, it speculates that issues around aging, diminishment, and the lack of involvement by bishops might be related to the bishops' concerns. On the other hand, the interviews might be considered a more reliable indicator of the bishops' experiences with women religious and their institutes. Comments such as "I appreciate them for who they are," or "[t]hey were willing to go to places that were small . . . with hardly any resources . . . [T]hey may not have the visibility, but they have the impact" reflect the bishops' appreciation for the contributions of women religious.

I would have appreciated more on collaboration with women, both lay and religious, since this is an area to which the bishops gave significant attention in the 1990s and early 2000s in their pastoral reflection on women

---

1. Pope Francis, *Apostolic Exhortation Evangelii Gaudium*, November 24, 2013, https://w2.vatican.va/content/francesco/en/apost_exhortations/documents/papa-francesco_esortazione-ap_20131124_evangelii-gaudium.html.

in the Church and in society, *Strengthening the Bonds of Peace,* and the reflection on the role of women in the Church, in *From Words to Deeds* by the bishops' Committee on Women in Society and the Church.[2] Recognizing and including women and men religious as collaborators and/or advisors, along with the commonly mentioned individuals and groups with whom bishops collaborate and consult, could assist bishops in exercising their governance role and their pastoral ministry to the people of the diocese. Pope John Paul II, in the 2003 apostolic exhortation *Pastores gregis,* situated a bishop's pastoral style of governance within a "lived ecclesial communion" as increasingly open to collaboration with all (PG 44).

Since the promulgation of the revised Code of Canon Law 35 years ago, the bishops in the United States have recognized an increased role for lay persons in the life of the Church. Specifically, the Code opened to women and lay men positions that had previous been held only by priests, such as chancellor, tribunal judge, and promotor of justice. The survey report acknowledges, for example, that the first persons to be appointed to the new possibility for pastoral leadership permitted by canon 517§2 (entrusting a participation in the pastoral care of a parish to a lay person or a deacon), most commonly referred to as Parish Life Coordinators, were women religious who were later followed by lay men and women. Today the emergence of lay women and men as Lay Ecclesial Ministers has changed the ecclesiastical landscape in this country and at the same time presented its own challenges for bishops, especially regarding clarity of roles and responsibilities. With greater clarity on functions and roles, the broadening of ministerial opportunities and the recognition of the many gifts of the Spirit in service to the Church bodes well for the future of parish and diocesan ministry.

Several of the bishops' preferences reported in the data are based on the self-identification of individual bishop participants along theological lines as traditional, moderate, or progressive. I did not find this characterization particularly helpful in contrasting styles, reading materials, or news programs. It seems potentially to contribute to an over-emphasis on

---

2. United States Conference of Catholic Bishops, *Strengthening the Bonds of Peace,* November, 1994, http://www.usccb.org/about/laity-marriage-family-life-and-youth/womens-issues/strengthening-the-bonds-of-peace.cfm.

United States Conference of Bishops, *From Words to Deeds: Continuing Reflections on the Role of Women in the Church,* September 15, 1998, http://www.usccb.org/about/laity-marriage-family-life-and-youth/womens-issues/from-words-to-deeds.cfm.

polarities rather than similarities, perhaps drawing lines that divide rather than elements that unify. It is even difficult to know where along the spectrum one might self-identify, such as "almost moderate" or "almost progressive" or even a combination of categories.

I am grateful to CARA for this report, and especially to the bishops who participated in the survey. No single survey can adequately tell the whole story about the life and ministry of bishops. However, I was delighted that the data reported in the CARA survey confirmed my experience of working with bishops for over 30 years in church management and church institutions. From a unique vantage point while at the Bishops' Conference, I could observe the profoundly good and generous spirit of many of the bishops guiding our Church. The CARA data confirms today that, simply from the perspective of sheer hard work, the U.S. bishops dedicate themselves with great devotion to carrying out their administrative responsibilities and providing pastoral service to those entrusted to their care. For this, we should all give thanks.

Thomas J. Reese, SJ

Anyone who wants to be a bishop needs their head examined is the only conclusion you can reach after reading the first seven chapters of this book. Here is a job where you get only 6.5 hours of sleep per night, 2.1 hours less or 24 percent less than the American average. Sleep deprivation is known to have deleterious effects on one's health.

And what do they do while they are awake? Work. Work. Work. After spending 78 minutes keeping up on the news, they then work 9.8 hours a day, 2.2 hours more than the average worker of their age. Of this time, 4.5 hours are spent in their offices, 3.4 hours in attending meetings, and 1.9 hours attending events. Nor do they get weekends off. Bishops on average report working 6.3 days a week. This all adds up to a 62.5-hour work week. In short, "the average Catholic bishop in the United States today is quite

Father Thomas Reese is a Jesuit priest who holds a doctorate in political science. He was editor of *America* magazine and a senior fellow at the Woodstock Theological Center when he wrote *Archbishop: Inside the Power Structure of the American Catholic Church* (1989), *A Flock of Shepherds: The National Conference of Catholic Bishops* (1992), and *Inside the Vatican: The Politics and Organization of the Catholic Church* (1996). Father Reese is currently a senior analyst for Religion News Service and a member of the U.S. Commission on International Religious Freedom.

the workaholic sacrificing on average two hours of sleep a night in order to keep up with all of his responsibilities."

What is amazing is that they actually like their jobs. More than three out of five (63 percent) said that they "strongly" agreed that "I am satisfied with my life as bishop." Another third (34 percent) agreed "somewhat." Only three percent "strongly" agreed that burnout was a problem.

Perhaps the fact that they spend an average of 108 minutes a day in prayer helps (including meditation, Mass, the Divine Office, the Rosary, and other devotions). They also find great satisfaction in administering the sacraments, preaching the Word, and being part of a Christian community working together to share the Good News of the Gospel.

On the other hand, only 43 percent found the same satisfaction in organizing and administering the work of the church. Since almost eight hours a day are spent in the office or in meetings, it is a surprise that they are as happy as they are in their work. One must conclude that the high they get from the pastoral side of their work overwhelms the negative experience of office work and meetings. Anecdotal support for this conclusion comes from retired bishops I interviewed who report that they would have retired earlier if they had known how much fun they would have doing pastoral work with no administrative responsibilities.

While I have great admiration for the dedication and hard work of the bishops, I fear that this study supports the view that the vision of most bishops is very narrow. The researchers report that "more than twice as many bishops described themselves as theologically 'traditional' compared to 'progressive.'" Almost half (47 percent) of the bishops report watching the news on the FOX Network, as compared to 21 percent for the American public.[3]

Sadly, only 38 percent say that engaging in efforts at social reform is of great importance as a source of satisfaction. This ranks eighth—even after organizing and administering the work of the church—of nine items presented to the bishops. What happened to Pope Francis' vision of a poor Church for the poor?

Just as shocking is that only 16 percent of the bishops mentioned Pope Francis as one of three aspects of the Church in the United States today that gives them the greatest hope. "Youth and young adults," "laity,"

---

3. Pew Research Center U.S. Politics & Policy, "In Changing News Landscape, Even Television is Vulnerable: Trends in News Consumption: 1991–2012," September 27, 2012, http://www.people-press.org/2012/09/27/in-changing-news-landscape-even-television-is-vulnerable/.

"spirituality and sacraments," "priests," and "vocations and seminarians" ranked higher.

The hope placed in youth and young adults is a bit surprising granted the large numbers abandoning the Church. Perhaps the slice of young people with whom the bishops meet is more conservative and pious than their peers, who although raised Catholic are in large numbers no longer identifying as Catholics. Perhaps this is a major problem for bishops—they mainly hear from those who agree with them.

When asked about the challenges facing the Church in the United States, the top five responses were "secularism" and "religious freedom," followed by "indifference, loss of faith, non-practicing," "marriage and family," and "lack of priests, vocations" in a virtual tie.

One gets the impression there is little self-critical thinking here. All the problems are outside the Church. "When asked, practically all bishops, some 95 percent, agreed "somewhat" or "strongly" that 'secular U.S. culture is hostile to the values of Catholicism.'" It is the world that must change, not the Church.

One wonders how they would respond to Pope Francis' words to the Latin American bishops about why people have left the Church:

> Perhaps the Church appeared too weak, perhaps too distant from their needs, perhaps too poor to respond to their concerns, perhaps too cold, perhaps too caught up with itself, perhaps a prisoner of its own rigid formulas, perhaps the world seems to have made the Church a relic of the past, unfit for new questions; perhaps the Church could speak to people in their infancy but not to those come of age.

Do the bishops agree with Pope Francis that "we lose people because they don't understand what we are saying, because we have forgotten the language of simplicity and import an intellectualism foreign to our people"? How about the Church as a field hospital?

The researchers quite rightly focus on the relationship of the bishop to his priests, who are his closest collaborators. Here we find that "Nearly nine in ten bishops reported that the 'limited number of available priests' is "somewhat" or "a great" administrative issue in their diocese." This is not surprising when CARA reports that "Twenty years ago the ratio of Catholics per diocesan priest was 1,774 and in 2016 it had grown to 2,628."

In addition, about 60 percent of the bishops say that "criticism from laity about priests" is a day-to-day problem. So the problem is not only quantity but quality. Pope Francis has been very vocal in his criticism of clericalism among priests and bishops.

It is not surprising then when 75 percent of bishops reported that priest personnel issues were "somewhat" or "a great" problem. Sixty-four percent of the bishops identify working with international priests as "somewhat" or "a great" problem, so that will not solve their personnel problems. The fact that priests cannot be easily fired or replaced provides a unique HR problem for bishops that is not faced by other CEOs.

There is little indication, however, that the American bishops are likely to ask Pope Francis for permission to ordain married men, despite the many news reports indicating that he would consider this if asked by a bishops' conference. Rather the preferred solution to the shortage appears to be more priests being pastors of multiple parishes. In urban areas, parishes will continue to be closed or merged, while in rural areas, parish coordinators will become more common.

The number of parish coordinators has declined since a high of 565 in 2003 to 369 in 2015, closely tracking the plummeting fall in the number of sister coordinators during the same period (Figure 6.2). The number of deacon coordinators has grown, but not enough to make up for the loss of sisters.

The CARA researchers believe that "looking ahead to the next five years, using non-priest leaders is the strategy that is likely to show the greatest increase in use," with progressive bishops being more likely than moderates or traditional bishops to have used, or be willing to use, non-priest leaders.

Most bishops do agree (90 percent) that "women should have more leadership roles in parishes" and (80 percent) "in my diocese." On the other hand, one-fifth of the bishops indicated that working with women's religious orders was "somewhat" or "a great" problem.

Although bishops often tout their women chancellors as an example of female empowerment in the church, these positions have become less important with the creation of positions like moderator of the curia, finance director, and priest personnel director. The female chancellor is often little more than an office manager. The really important jobs available in dioceses to women are directors of Catholic Charities, superintendents of schools, and directors of finance, since the positions of vicar general, moderator of the curia, and priest personnel are only open to priests.

The CARA researchers also give attention to diocesan pastoral planning, but I must confess to being an agnostic when it comes to such plans. Often these plans are very general and aspirational with little detail on what is actually to be done. Often the process is more important than the product, but the process can be very important to the people who participate.

The final chapter deals with teaching, which most bishops consider an important part of their ministry. The data collected by CARA supports the impression that some bishops write more about the sanctity of life than about Catholic social teaching (Table 7.2). Thirty-eight percent wrote on sanctity of life on a regular basis as opposed to 24 percent writing about Catholic social teaching on a regular basis.

On the other hand, 66 percent of the bishops report writing on the two topics with approximately equal frequency. One-quarter say they write more about sanctity of life than Catholic social teaching, and only 9 percent say they do the opposite. Among self-described traditional bishops, 35 percent write about the sanctity of life more frequently than Catholic social teaching. The frequency with which bishops write about topics such as the sanctity of life or Catholic social teaching does not vary by whether they reside in a blue or red state.

The CARA researchers also present wonderful data on how bishops speak on political issues. Three-quarters of bishops say they have often or regularly asked Catholics to consider Catholic teaching when voting for candidates. Additionally, most bishops have often or regularly spoken to the general public about issues of the day.

Finally, as a journalist, I found it also fascinating to learn that:

About six in ten bishops say that criticism in the secular press or media is at least "somewhat" of a problem for them. The proportion is higher for those who live in relatively secular states and lower for those who live in relatively religious states. Bishops who describe themselves as theologically traditional are considerably more likely than progressives to describe such criticism as "a great" problem.

Despite these negative feelings toward the press, 65 percent of bishops said they have been interviewed on a local secular radio or television channel "often" or "on a regular basis" during the past five years. My colleagues in the media do not report such easy access to the bishops.

In conclusion, the CARA research shows that bishops are hardworking, dedicated, traditional men who would rather be doing pastoral work. It also shows that the priest shortage is reaching a critical stage, and the bishops have no good plan to deal with it. The conservative nature of these bishops is keeping them from thinking outside the box in order to respond to the priest shortage and to contemporary American culture.

CARA is to be commended for producing a fine report based on solid empirical data. Also to be thanked are the bishops who provided the data. We hope to see more such research in the future.

Joseph William Cardinal Tobin, CSsR

My childhood years spanned the late 1950s into the early 1960s. Television offered little kids a steady diet of family sitcoms, built around the bread-winning Dad and the stay-at-home Mom. As a young boy, I couldn't help but compare my father to the dads on *Leave It to Beaver, My Three Sons,* or *Father Knows Best.*

I noted that the TV patriarchs returned home each night with a brief-case, stuffed with "papers from the office." My father, a cost analyst for an automaker, never did. If he brought anything with him, it was usually some article of clothing he found on sale during his lunch hour, which he often spent browsing through a discount store across the street from his office, driven by the Sisyphean task of outfitting his ever-expanding brood. (I am the eldest of 13 children.)

The absence of the briefcase bothered me, so one day I asked him why he did not bring home paperwork from the office. "Because I married your mother. I didn't marry General Motors," was his succinct reply.

Like my father, bishops wear a ring. In the history of the Latin Church, this symbol was commonly regarded as emblematic of the mystical be-trothal of the bishop to his church. Historians recall ecclesiastical decrees stipulating that "a bishop deserting the Church to which he was consecrated

---

Cardinal Tobin is a member of the Redemptorist community and served as Superior General of the Redemptorists in Rome from 1997 until 2009. In 2010, Pope Benedict XVI named Father Tobin to the Roman Curia post of Secretary of the Congregation for Institutes of Consecrated Life and Societies of Apostolic Life (CICLSA). Two years later, Pope Benedict XVI appointed him Archbishop of Indianapolis. Pope Francis named him to the College of Cardinals in 2016. He has participated in five Synods of Bishops, and has been a member of the Canon Law Society of America since 1985. In November 2016, Pope Francis appointed him to serve as the Archbishop of Newark.

and transferring himself to another is to be held guilty of adultery and is to be visited with the same penalties as a man who, forsaking his own wife, goes to live with another woman."[4] I do not know how those decretalists would judge the transfer of bishops today.

The notion of betrothal may contribute to understanding some of the data collected by CARA in this thought-provoking book. Compared to priests as well as their contemporaries in the secular world, bishops in the United States describe working longer hours over a career that extends significantly more years beyond the customary age for retirement. Curiously, bishops express greater job satisfaction than priests, though many observers would certainly wonder why.

A bishop's peculiar relationship to the diocese is different from my father's connection to General Motors and certainly is closer to what Dad felt for his family. I am not alone in that sentiment. During a visit to Buenos Aires in 2007, I read a newspaper interview with the local archbishop, Jorge Bergoglio. The journalist referred to a rumor that the conclave of 2005 had nearly chosen him to succeed Pope John Paul II and asked whether the Archbishop was disappointed. "Absolutely not," was his vehement reply. "I would die without my people."

My personal experience as well as conversations with brothers in episcopal ministry convince me that responsibility for *my people* is the most significant element in the self-understanding of a bishop. That self-understanding does not excuse myopia, even blindness regarding those who share the household of faith—let alone those on the margins who, almost by definition, are difficult to see without careful scrutiny and assiduous search. This volume suggests such myopia, if the widespread concerns of bishops remain a parade of *isms*: secularism, materialism, individualism, consumerism, relativism, etc. . . . Contrary to the testimony of some participants in the survey, the so-called "none's" are not necessarily unbelievers but rather the unaligned, who frequently describe themselves as "spiritual, not religious."

I wonder if we bishops are able to look beyond categories and into hearts in order to understand why ideas and lifestyles are so attractive to people, *our people*. We should not be quick to identify too easily with Paul and grouse that "the time has come when people will not tolerate sound doctrine but, following their own desires and insatiable curiosity,

---

4. Andre' Du Saussay, *Panoplia Episcopalis* (Paris, 1646), 175–294.

will accumulate teachers and will stop listening to the truth and will be diverted to myths" (2 Timothy 4, 3–4). Even if the ninety-nine number less than before, the shepherd still must look for the one (or more) who are lost and spare no effort to bring them back.

His experience of personal love and responsibility for the people entrusted to him can explain why the bishop spends long hours in administrative tasks as well as private prayer. Yet, when he receives his ring from the one who presides at his ordination, he hears the words: "Receive this ring, the seal of fidelity: adorned with undefiled faith, preserve unblemished the bride of God, the Holy Church." The "bride" is neither his nor coextensive with his diocese. The ring symbolizes his faithful responsibility for the whole, Holy Church. When Jesus commissions Peter with pastoral authority, it is not given to feed *Peter's* sheep. The people of God always remain God's.

While I was interested in the profile of bishops, I was disappointed by the underdeveloped portion of the survey that examined the collective responsibility shared by bishops as members of a College. In the judgment of the authors of the report, the congruence between the priorities of the national pastoral plan and themes in some diocesan plans may suggest some collaboration, interaction, or exchanging of ideas between bishops regarding the way forward. I would have liked to hear more about the experience of collegiality in different arenas, such as the ecclesiastical province as well as the national conference. Three reasons underscore the crucial significance of these relationships.

First, the Church appears to have discovered new value in discernment. The Second Vatican Council recalled that the Church has always had "the duty of scrutinizing the signs of the times and of interpreting them in the light of the Gospel."[5] The interpretation is not given a priori; rather the Church "labors to decipher authentic signs of God's presence and purpose in the happenings, needs and desires in which this People has a part along with other men of our age."[6]

At the universal level, the Church recognizes the difficult but necessary work of discernment. For example, the *Lineamenta*, a preparatory document for the 2012 Synod of Bishops on the new evangelization and

---

5. Second Vatican Council, "*Pastoral Constitution on the Church in the Modern World, Gaudium et Spes*" (1965), http://www.vatican.va/archive/hist_councils/ii_vatican_council/documents/vat-ii_cons_19651207_gaudium-et-spes_en.html.

6. Ibid.

transmission of faith, used the word "discernment" 24 times. The subsequent *Instrumentum Laboris* or working document for that Synod reduced that number to 10, but still argued that the way forward for the Church was not following a set of self-evident principles, but rather "a process of discernment, which can also serve as a way of responding to the current situation with greater courage and responsibility."[7] Although the report notes the bishop's use of consultative bodies in his diocese, I wonder to what degree the assembly of the USCCB or the meetings of an ecclesiastical province can be forums for discernment. The rapidity and depth of cultural change calls for a more intentional process of discernment and action by those charged with pastoral leadership.

Second, it is clear that Pope Francis is trying to reimagine the work of bishops on a foundation of greater collegiality and synodality. He has transferred to national episcopal conferences some functions that formerly had been the exclusive purvey of the departments of the Roman Curia, such as the translation of liturgical texts into the vernacular. He has indicated his willingness to consider the ordination of married men, the so-called *viri probati*, if an episcopal conference makes the requests.

His reluctance to respond to public challenges to magisterial statements like the apostolic exhortation, *Amoris Laetitia*, by a few bishops and cardinals may be due, in part, to his expectation that bishops meet to study the orientation given and discern how best to apply the principles in the local Churches that have been entrusted to their care.

While Pope Francis has continued to use the annual celebration of Saints Peter and Paul to bless the *pallia*, an ancient symbol for the office of a metropolitan archbishop, four years ago he ceased to impose the vestment in the Vatican basilica. Instead, he has stipulated that the nuncio impose the pallium on the shoulders of the archbishop in his metropolitan cathedral with the participation of the Ordinaries of the suffragan dioceses. I believe this change is an effort to revive the significance of the *metropolis*, an ancient configuration of an archdiocese and neighboring sees that played a crucial role in governance in the first millennia of Christianity.

Third, the communion of bishops in study, prayerful discernment, and effective action will be a prophetic and countercultural sign in the polarized landscape of the United States. The survey asked the bishops to self-identify their general theological orientation on a spectrum from very

---

7. Synod of Bishops, XIII Ordinary General Assembly, *The New Evangelization for the Transmission of the Christian Faith*, Instrumentum Laboris (Vatican City, 2012), 16.

traditional to very progressive; unfortunately this can play into an uncritical assumption of a popular narrative that features a "red state–blue state–purple state" paradigm. The limits of this way of thinking are not simply that reported preferences in news sources or theological opinions can lead to generalizations that border on caricatures. What is more insidious is the temptation to believe that bishops who read different magazines or watch dissimilar newscasts can do no better than manage a peaceful, albeit superficial, coexistence. Lest I appear alarmist, one should recognize the paralysis of the Congress, the acrimony of social media, and progressive fragmentation of American life.

The courageous testimony of bishops who together wrestle with reading the "signs of times and places" in the light of the Gospel can be a welcome, even surprising alternative to the social shibboleths that stifle dialogue in the public square.

Catholic Bishops in the United States provides a snapshot of the men who are chosen to lead the Catholic Church in the United States in the first decades of this new millennium. I hope that the reading of these pages will lead to a deeper understanding of the love and the responsibility we feel for the portion of the Vineyard that has been entrusted to our care. The ring each of us wears calls us to faithful service of a particular Church but also for the entire Bride of God. Hence, as disciples we should be interested how bishops experience collegiality in their corporate duty to care for the national and universal Church.

 CARA Survey of U.S. Catholic Bishops

Center for Applied Research in the Apostolate at Georgetown University

DIRECTIONS: Please fill out this questionnaire and return it in the envelope provided. To maintain the confidentiality of your response, return the postcard separately to let us know that you have completed the survey. **If a question does not apply to you or you do not know how to respond, please leave it blank.** Please note that "Diocese" is used here as a generic reference to both Archdiocese and Diocese.

There are many sources of satisfaction in the life and work of a bishop. Please indicate how important each of the following is as a source of satisfaction to you. *Please use these responses for questions 1–9.*

| 1 = No importance | 3 = Some importance |
| 2 = Little importance | 4 = Great importance |

1	2	3	4	
☐	☐	☐	☐	1. Joy of administering the sacraments and presiding over the liturgy.
☐	☐	☐	☐	2. Respect that comes to the episcopal office.
☐	☐	☐	☐	3. Organizing and administering the work of the Church.
☐	☐	☐	☐	4. Challenge of being the leader of a Catholic Christian community.
☐	☐	☐	☐	5. Engaging in efforts at social reform.
☐	☐	☐	☐	6. Serving as *alter Christus* to the faithful.
☐	☐	☐	☐	7. Being part of a community of Christians who are working together to share the Good News of the Gospel.
☐	☐	☐	☐	8. Opportunity to work with many people and be a part of their lives.
☐	☐	☐	☐	9. Satisfaction of preaching the Word.

Please use the following responses for questions 10–31.

1 = **No problem at all**   3 = **Somewhat of a problem**
2 = **Very little problem**   4 = **A great problem**

How much are each of the following a problem to you on a day-to-day basis?

1	2	3	4	
☐	☐	☐	☐	10. Theological divisions among my priests.
☐	☐	☐	☐	11. Unrealistic demands and expectations of lay people.
☐	☐	☐	☐	12. Conflict with parishioners or laity about issues of the day.
☐	☐	☐	☐	13. Difficulty of really reaching people today.
☐	☐	☐	☐	14. Loneliness of priestly/episcopal life.
☐	☐	☐	☐	15. Too much work.
☐	☐	☐	☐	16. The way authority is exercised in the Church.
☐	☐	☐	☐	17. The image of the priesthood today.
☐	☐	☐	☐	18. The image of bishops today.
☐	☐	☐	☐	19. Criticism from priests.
☐	☐	☐	☐	20. Criticism from laity about priests.
☐	☐	☐	☐	21. Criticism in the secular press or media.

How much of a problem are these administrative issues to you on a day-to-day basis?

1	2	3	4	
☐	☐	☐	☐	22. Limited number of available priests.
☐	☐	☐	☐	23. Working with international priests.
☐	☐	☐	☐	24. Working with men's religious orders.
☐	☐	☐	☐	25. Working with women's religious orders.
☐	☐	☐	☐	26. Parish restructuring in the diocese.
☐	☐	☐	☐	27. The diocesan financial situation.
☐	☐	☐	☐	28. Diocesan legal issues.
☐	☐	☐	☐	29. Priest morale.
☐	☐	☐	☐	30. Priest personnel issues.
☐	☐	☐	☐	31. Non-priest diocesan personnel issues.

In the **last** five years, to what extent have you used these strategies to address the limited number of priests to lead parishes? *Use these responses for questions 32–37.*

ɪ = **Not at all**   3 = **Somewhat**
2 = **Not very much** 4 = **A fair amount**

ɪ	2	3	4	
☐	☐	☐	☐	32. One priest leads multiple parishes (c526.1).
☐	☐	☐	☐	33. Non-priests lead some parishes with a priest sacramental minister (c517.2).
☐	☐	☐	☐	34. Close or merge parishes.
☐	☐	☐	☐	35. Increase retirement age for priests.
☐	☐	☐	☐	36. Increase use of international priests.
☐	☐	☐	☐	37. Increase local vocation efforts.

In the **next** five years, how likely would you be to use the same strategies to address the limited number of priests to lead parishes? *Use these responses for questions 38–43.*

ɪ = **Not likely at all** 3 = **Somewhat likely**
2 = **Not very likely**   4 = **Very likely**

ɪ	2	3	4	
☐	☐	☐	☐	38. One priest leads multiple parishes (c526.1).
☐	☐	☐	☐	39. Non-priests lead some parishes with a priest sacramental minister (c517.2).
☐	☐	☐	☐	40. Close or merge parishes.
☐	☐	☐	☐	41. Increase retirement age for priests.
☐	☐	☐	☐	42. Increase use of international priests.
☐	☐	☐	☐	43. Increase local vocation efforts.

Yes	No	
☐	☐	44. Do you write a personal blog?
☐	☐	45. Do you have your own Facebook page?

Please use these responses for questions 46–67.

1 = Disagree strongly   3 = Agree somewhat
2 = Disagree somewhat   4 = Agree strongly

1	2	3	4	
☐	☐	☐	☐	46. I am too busy to pray as much as I would like.
☐	☐	☐	☐	47. I am satisfied with my life as a bishop.
☐	☐	☐	☐	48. I would be happier if I could focus on my pastoral ministry and let others do administrative work.
☐	☐	☐	☐	49. I frequently feel burned out.
☐	☐	☐	☐	50. I wish to spend more time with other priests in the diocese.
☐	☐	☐	☐	51. I am too busy to personally counsel and pastor all the priests of my diocese.
☐	☐	☐	☐	52. I feel my current diocese is my home.
☐	☐	☐	☐	53. I feel accepted by most priests of my current diocese.
☐	☐	☐	☐	54. Most of my closest priest friends are priests of my current diocese.
☐	☐	☐	☐	55. Other bishops are among my closest friends.
☐	☐	☐	☐	56. I support bringing more international priests into the diocese.
☐	☐	☐	☐	57. It is essential to uphold the distinction between priests and laity in the Church.
☐	☐	☐	☐	58. Catholic laity are sufficiently respectful of the priest's authority.
☐	☐	☐	☐	59. Priests are sufficiently respectful of the voice of the laity.
☐	☐	☐	☐	60. Priests in a diocese should have greater input in suggesting names for the office of bishop.
☐	☐	☐	☐	61. It is important to me to be a spokesman for Catholicism in my diocese.
☐	☐	☐	☐	62. As a bishop I have a special responsibility beyond that of other priests for preserving and upholding the faith.
☐	☐	☐	☐	63. Secular U.S. culture is hostile to the values of Catholicism.
☐	☐	☐	☐	64. The Catholic Church's right to religious freedom faces increasing threat from the government.
☐	☐	☐	☐	65. Women should have more leadership roles in parishes.
☐	☐	☐	☐	66. Women should have more leadership roles in my diocese.
☐	☐	☐	☐	67. Media coverage of clergy sexual abuse has made it challenging to present or defend Church teachings in my diocese.

In the absence of an available priest, how do you feel about appointing the following to lead parishes (c517.2). *Please use these responses for questions 68–72.*

1 = **Not willing at all**   3 = **Somewhat willing**
2 = **Not very willing**   4 = **Very willing**

1	2	3	4	
☐	☐	☐	☐	68. Permanent Deacon.
☐	☐	☐	☐	69. Religious Sister.
☐	☐	☐	☐	70. Religious Brother.
☐	☐	☐	☐	71. Lay Man.
☐	☐	☐	☐	72. Lay Woman.

How would you describe diocesan-wide policies related to parish operations in the following areas? *Please use these responses for questions 73–77.*

1 = **No diocesan policy**   3 = **Specific guidelines in key areas**
2 = **General guidelines**   4 = **Detailed/highly standardized**

1	2	3	4	
☐	☐	☐	☐	73. Liturgy.
☐	☐	☐	☐	74. Sacramental preparation.
☐	☐	☐	☐	75. Finances.
☐	☐	☐	☐	76. Personnel management.
☐	☐	☐	☐	77. Religious education.

Please use these responses for questions 78–89.

1 = **Never**   3 = **Often**
2 = **Occasionally** 4 = **On a regular basis**

In the last five years, how often have you written to Catholics (e.g., a pastoral letter or column in the diocesan newspaper) on these topics?

1	2	3	4	
☐	☐	☐	☐	78. Spiritual or Biblical reflection.
☐	☐	☐	☐	79. Catholic theology.
☐	☐	☐	☐	80. Catholic teaching on the family.
☐	☐	☐	☐	81. Catholic teaching on sexual morality.
☐	☐	☐	☐	82. Catholic teaching on sanctity of life.
☐	☐	☐	☐	83. Catholic social teaching.
☐	☐	☐	☐	84. Religious freedom issues.

In the last five years, how often have you?

☐ ☐ ☐ ☐ 85. Asked Catholics to vote a particular way on a ballot initiative or referendum.

☐ ☐ ☐ ☐ 86. Asked Catholics to consider Catholic teaching when voting for candidates.

☐ ☐ ☐ ☐ 87. Made statements to the general public about current social or political issues.

☐ ☐ ☐ ☐ 88. Lobbied lawmakers or other political leaders about law or policy.

☐ ☐ ☐ ☐ 89. Been interviewed on a local secular radio or television channel.

90. In what USCCB region is your current diocese? _____

91. How much media coverage, either local or national, was directed at your **current** diocese in the wake of the revelations of clergy sexual abuse in the Church?
☐ Little or no coverage.
☐ Some coverage.
☐ A large amount of coverage.
☐ Extensive coverage.

Yes   **No**

☐   ☐   92. Were you in ministry in your **current** diocese in the wake of the revelations of clergy sexual abuse?

☐   ☐   93. Were you born in the United States?

☐   ☐   94. Did you grow up in your current diocese?

☐   ☐   95. Are you a member of a religious order?

☐   ☐   96. Did you attend a high school seminary?

☐   ☐   97. Do you currently have a spiritual director?

☐   ☐   98. Did you make a personal retreat last year?

☐   ☐   99. Are you retired?

☐   ☐   100. *If retired*, are you still active in ministry?

101. Which best describes your current (or, if retired, emeritus) role in the Church?
☐ Archbishop with (an) auxiliary bishop(s).
☐ Archbishop without an auxiliary bishop.
☐ Bishop with (an) auxiliary bishop(s).
☐ Bishop without an auxiliary bishop.
☐ Auxiliary bishop.

102. Year you were born: _____

103. Which one category best describes your primary racial or ethnic background?
    ☐ African / African-American / black.
    ☐ Native American / Alaska Native.
    ☐ Asian / Pacific Islander / Native Hawaiian.
    ☐ Caucasian / European American / white.
    ☐ Hispanic / Latino.
    ☐ Other (describe:) _____

104. What kind of undergraduate college did you attend?
    ☐ Diocesan seminary. ☐ Other private.
    ☐ Catholic college.   ☐ Public.

105. Please list any Graduate Degrees (M.A., M.Div., Ph.D., S.T.D., etc.) and the University attended:
    Degree University

    _____   _____

    _____   _____

    _____   _____

106. Year you were ordained to priesthood: _____

107. Prior to episcopacy, how many years were you a: _____

    ___ Parochial vicar?   ___ Bishop's secretary?
    ___ Pastor?   ___ Chancellor?
    ___ Professor?   ___ Other position in chancery?
    ___ Vice Rector?   ___ Vicar general?
    ___ Rector?   ___ Diocesan administrator?
    ___ Other? _____

108. Year you were ordained to the episcopacy: _____

109. Year appointed to your current (if retired, emeritus) position: _____

110. Your prior experience as a bishop:

    ☐ Auxiliary in current diocese.
    ☐ Auxiliary in a different diocese.
    ☐ Ordinary in a different diocese.
    ☐ No prior experience as bishop.

111. During an average month, how many days are you outside your diocese for conferences, meetings, or other similar events? _____

112. Approximate number of Confirmation celebrations at which you officiated during last twelve months: _____

113. Approximate number of parishes you visited (not counting Confirmation ceremonies) during last twelve months: _____

114. *If active in ministry:* Typical number of days you work each week. _____

115. *If active in ministry:* Typical number of hours you work each week. _____

116. *If active in ministry:* Weeks of vacation you took last year. _____

117. Understanding that there is no typical day, on average, how many hours a day (*you may use fractional numbers*) do you spend . . .
   ___ Sleeping?
   ___ Praying (including Mass)?
   ___ Exercising?
   ___ Attending meetings?
   ___ Working in your office?
   ___ Reading/watching news?
   ___ Traveling?
   ___ Attending a parish, diocesan, or civic function?
   ___ Doing other miscellaneous things for yourself or others?

118. What national secular newspaper(s) do you read on a regular basis?

   ☐ *New York Times*   ☐ *Wall Street Journal*
   ☐ *USA Today*   ☐ *Washington Post*
   ☐ Local newspaper   ☐ Other: _____

119. What religious newspapers or magazines do you read on a regular basis?

   ☐ *National Catholic Register*
   ☐ *National Catholic Reporter*
   ☐ *America*   ☐ *Our Sunday Visitor*
   ☐ *Commonweal*   ☐ *The Wanderer*
   ☐ *First Things*   ☐ Other: _____

120. Your preferred TV channel to watch national news:

   ☐ ABC   ☐ CBS   ☐ CNN   ☐ FOX News
   ☐ MSNBC ☐ NBC ☐ Other: _____

121. How would others describe your general theological orientation?

   ☐ Very traditional.
   ☐ Moderately traditional.
   ☐ Moderate.
   ☐ Moderately progressive.
   ☐ Very progressive.

122. Bishops fulfill many essential roles in the life of the Church in their dioceses and in the nation. Which three roles are most important to you?

   _____
   _____
   _____

123. What three aspects of the Church in the U.S. today give you the greatest amount of hope?

_____

_____

_____

124. What do you perceive as the three greatest challenges to the Church in the U.S. today?

_____

_____

_____

125. I have a personal email address that only I access.

☐ Yes ☐ No

126. Regarding my office email address:

☐ Only I have access to it.
☐ My secretary monitors it for me.
☐ I do not have an office email.

127. In general, how can the priests of your diocese reach you by email?

☐ Through my personal email address.
☐ Through my office email address.
☐ Through my secretary's email address.
☐ Other: _____

128. In general, how can the priests of your diocese reach you by phone?

☐ They call or text my personal cell phone.
☐ They call the secretary at my office.
☐ Other: _____

For questions 129 to 137, you can either indicate the name of your diocese (_____) and we will look up the information or you can fill out the questions below. In either case, we will guard your confidentiality. You may delegate these last questions to your assistant.

129. Approximate number of Catholics in your diocese:

_____

130. Approximate percentage of Catholics compared to total population in your diocese: _____

131. Number of parishes in your diocese: _____

132. Approximate number of active diocesan priests serving in your diocese:

_____

133. Of the active diocesan priests, approximately what percentage are foreign born? _____

134. Of these foreign-born priests, approximate what percentage are incardinated in your diocese? _____

135. Approximate number of retired diocesan priests in your diocese: _____

136. Approximate number of active religious order priests in your diocese: _____

137. Approximate number of retired religious order priests in your diocese: _____

Thank you for completing this survey.

Center for Applied Research in the Apostolate (CARA)
2300 Wisconsin Ave NW, Suite 400
Washington, DC 20007
Phone: (202) 687-8080 Fax: (202) 687-8083

Survey Response Analysis

Table B.1 shows comparisons between survey respondents and non-respondents on a variety of bishop and diocesan characteristics. The only significant difference is related to the size of the diocese. Respondents were more likely to be from smaller dioceses than from larger ones.

Table B.1 Comparison of Bishops who Responded to the Survey with Non-Responding Bishops

	All Latin Rite Ordinaries[a] (%)	Survey Respondents (%)	Non-Respondents (%)
Type of priest			
Diocesan	90	92	86
Religious order	10	8	14
Type of ordinary			
Bishop	82	82	82
Archbishop	18	18	18
Race			
White (not Hispanic)	88	90	82
Other	12	10	18

(continued)

Table B.1 Continued

	All Latin Rite Ordinaries[a] (%)	Survey Respondents (%)	Non-Respondents (%)
Ordination (to priesthood) cohort			
Vatican II (1964–1977)	49	50	48
Post–Vatican II (1978–1991)	43	44	40
Jubilee (1992–2003)	8	6	12
Decade ordained to episcopacy			
1980s	7	6	10
1990s	21	20	24
2000s	45	46	40
2010s	27	27	26
Appointed by			
Pope John Paul II	51	50	56
Pope Benedict XVI	37	40	30
Pope Francis	11	10	14
Number of Catholics in the diocese[b]			
Fewer than 100,000	29	31	24
100,000 to 249,999	30	35	20
250,000 to 999,999	30	27	35
One million or more	11	6	22
Major census region			
Northeast	18	18	20
South	31	33	25
Midwest	30	27	37
West	21	22	18

[a] Only ordinaries leading territorial (arch)dioceses.

[b] Differences between survey respondents and non-responders are statistically significant.

Source: Data from 2016 *Official Catholic Directory* and CARA Survey of Bishops, 2016.

APPENDIX C

Comparing Active Latin Rite to Other Bishops

The analyses in the main chapters of this book focused on the active Latin Rite ordinaries. The tables in this appendix show comparisons with the three other types of bishops included in the survey: active Latin Rite auxiliary, retired Latin Rite, and Eastern Rite.

Chapter 1: Who Are the Bishops and Where Do They Come From?

Table C1.1 Comparing Different Types of Bishops on Personal and Diocesan Characteristics

Characteristic	Active Latin Rite Ordinary (%)	Latin Rite Auxiliary (%)	Retired Latin Rite (%)	Eastern Rite (%)
Theological orientation*				
Traditional	42	38	18	83
Moderate	41	56	41	17
Progressive	17	6	41	0
Diocesan size*				
Small (Under 100K)	33	0	14	100
Medium (100K–249K)	33	7	21	0
Large (250K–999K)	29	36	33	0
Very large (Over a million)	6	58	31	0
State political orientation*				
Red	34	13	21	—
Purple	43	26	41	—
Blue	23	61	38	—
Birth cohort*				
Silent	23	15	95	33
Boomer	76	79	5	58
Gen X	2	6	0	8
Racial minority*	9	27	5	18
Pope appointed by*				
Paul VI	0	0	24	0
John Paul II	50	12	69	67
Benedict XVI	39	55	7	17
Francis	10	33	0	17

Table C1.1 Continued

Characteristic	Active Latin Rite Ordinary (%)	Latin Rite Auxiliary (%)	Retired Latin Rite (%)	Eastern Rite (%)
U.S. born*	97	76	86	42
Grew up in current diocese*	9	52	38	25
Member of a religious order	7	9	7	8
Attended high school seminary*	31	28	57	17
College type*				
Diocesan seminary	51	36	83	27
Catholic college	29	27	10	27
Public college	13	30	7	27
Other private college	6	6	0	18
Studied in Rome	48	23	34	55
Post-seminary education*	85	66	81	64
Higher education type*				
MDiv only	11	28	11	9
Theology	35	25	30	73
Canon law	26	19	11	0
Canon law & theology	2	0	3	0
Academic degree	14	22	24	0
Professional degree	12	6	22	18
Prior roles				
Parochial vicar*	93	87	88	58
Pastor	76	74	75	92
Vicar general	34	23	33	17
Professor	31	26	30	25
Seminary rector*	21	7	28	42
Chancellor	18	13	20	8
Bishop's secretary	16	10	20	8

*Differences between each type of responding bishop are statistically significant.
Source: CARA Survey of Bishops, 2016.

Chapter 2: A Day in the Life of a Bishop

Table C2.1 Comparing Different Types of Bishops on Activities

Activity	Active Latin Rite Ordinary	Latin Rite Auxiliary	Retired Latin Rite	Eastern Rite
Average Hours a Day Spent . . .				
Sleeping*	6.49	6.64	7.34	6.91
Praying*	1.80	1.83	2.54	1.91
Exercising*	0.49	0.48	0.76	0.68
Reading/watching news*	1.29	1.31	2.15	1.73
Working in the office*	4.49	4.19	2.73	5.95
Attending meetings*	3.44	3.35	0.89	1.68
Attending functions*	1.95	2.19	1.04	1.36
Average days worked each week*	6.33	6.31	5.44	6.33
Average hours worked each week*	50.97	51.29	24.94	44.41
Average confirmations in last year*	38.71	49.74	20.37	3.25
Average parish visits in last year*	35.7	30.87	17.04	18.45
Average vacation weeks in last year	2.96	2.53	2.89	2.06
Average days/month outside the diocese*	3.93	3.41	2.12	5.3

*Differences between each type of responding bishop are statistically significant.
Source: CARA Survey of Bishops, 2016.

Table C2.2 Comparison of Different Types of Bishops on Sources of News

News Source	Active Latin Rite Ordinary (%)	Latin Rite Auxiliary (%)	Retired Latin Rite (%)	Eastern Rite (%)
Secular newspapers read				
Local newspaper*	88	73	91	55
New York Times	37	20	31	36
Wall Street Journal	24	27	12	36
USA Today*	23	7	17	46
Washington Post*	6	23	0	0
Religious newspapers read				
National Catholic Register*	61	28	42	36
America*	60	48	88	18
First Things*	41	48	20	9
Commonweal*	38	7	39	9
Our Sunday Visitor	36	31	20	27
National Catholic Reporter	33	24	44	27
Television news watched				
Fox	46	39	35	33
CNN	35	27	23	33
CBS	16	4	13	11
NBC*	16	23	35	0
ABC	12	15	18	22
MSNBC	4	4	8	0

*Differences between each type of responding bishop are statistically significant.
Source: CARA Survey of Bishops, 2016.

Chapter 3: Satisfactions in Episcopal Life and Ministry

Table C3.1 Comparing Different Types of Bishops on Satisfactions

Satisfactions: Responded "Great Importance"	Active Latin Rite Ordinary (%)	Latin Rite Auxiliary (%)	Retired Latin Rite (%)	Eastern Rite (%)
Joy of administering the sacraments and presiding over the liturgy	97	100	98	92
Preaching the Word	89	91	86	100
Being part of a community of Christians who are working together to share the Good News of the Gospel	84	91	81	75
Opportunity to work with many people and be a part of their lives	77	94	76	75
Serving as an *alter Christus* to the faithful	73	81	71	82
Challenge of being leader of the Catholic Christian community	62	50	65	50
Organizing and administering the work of the church	43	38	43	50
Engaging in efforts at social reform	38	36	59	33
Respect that comes to the episcopal office*	7	21	7	17

*Differences between each type of responding bishop are statistically significant.
Source: CARA Survey of Bishops, 2016.

Chapter 4: Challenges, Hopes, Vocations

Table C4.1 Comparing Different Types of Bishops on Challenges Facing the Church

Challenge	Active Latin Rite Ordinary (%)	Latin Rite Auxiliary (%)	Retired Latin Rite (%)	Eastern Rite (%)
Secularism	45	27	47	50
Religious freedom	32	20	21	0
Indifference, loss of faith, non-practicing	15	17	13	30
Marriage and family	15	17	11	20
Lack of priests, vocations	13	13	24	0
Relativism	11	13	8	10

Source: CARA Survey of Bishops, 2016.

Table C4.2 Comparing Different Types of Bishops on Greatest Hopes for the Church

Greatest Hopes	Active Latin Rite Ordinary (%)	Latin Rite Auxiliary (%)	Retired Latin Rite (%)	Eastern Rite (%)
Youth and young adults*	51	50	16	18
Vocations and seminarians	28	13	22	27
Laity*	27	27	49	9
Priests	24	17	11	9
Spirituality and sacraments	23	17	35	27
Pope Francis*	16	20	38	9
Immigration, Hispanics, and diversity	15	17	8	9
Evangelization	15	17	14	0

*Differences between each type of responding bishop are statistically significant.
Source: CARA Survey of Bishops, 2016.

Chapter 5: Personnel and Collaboration

Table C5.1 Comparing Different Types of Bishops on Relationships with Priests

View on Relationships with Priests Responded: "Agree Strongly"	Active Latin Rite Ordinary (%)	Latin Rite Auxiliary (%)	Retired Latin Rite (%)	Eastern Rite (%)
I feel accepted by most priests of my diocese*	72	88	80	42
Other bishops are among my closest friends	27	16	43	33
I am too busy to personally counsel and pastor all the priests of my diocese	23	23	26	17
I wish to spend more time with other priests in the diocese	22	29	27	50
I support bringing more international priests into the diocese	14	13	13	46
Most of my closest priest friends are priests of my current diocese*	8	50	54	55

*Differences between each type of responding bishop are statistically significant.
Source: CARA Survey of Bishops, 2016.

Table C5.2 Comparing Different Types of Bishops on Personnel Problems

Problems Related to Personnel: Responded "A Great Problem"	Active Latin Rite Ordinary (%)	Latin Rite Auxiliary (%)	Retired Latin Rite (%)	Eastern Rite (%)
Limited available priests	52	55	50	33
Priest personnel issues	24	32	30	25
Working with international priests	15	23	11	0
Criticism from laity about priests	9	18	5	17
Theological differences among priests	6	6	5	0
Priest morale	3	13	3	17
Non-priest personnel issues	3	7	3	0
Working with women's religious orders	3	7	0	0
Criticism from priests	3	6	0	8
Working with men's religious orders	2	0	0	8

Source: CARA Survey of Bishops, 2016.

Chapter 6: Governance and Administration

Table C6.1 Comparing Different Types of Bishops on Strategies
for Addressing Priest Shortage

	Active Latin Rite Ordinary (%)	Latin Rite Auxiliary (%)	Retired Latin Rite (%)	Eastern Rite (%)
Last 5 Years—Used a Fair Amount				
Increase vocations	75	80	66	42
One priest multiple parishes	42	27	22	25
Increase international priests	24	23	22	50
Close or merge parishes	11	23	19	9
Non-priests lead some parishes	5	0	14	0
Increase retirement age	4	7	6	25
Next 5 Years—Very Likely to Use				
Increase vocations*	90	90	77	67
One priest multiple parishes*	44	36	41	17
Increase international priests	14	19	18	46
Close or merge parishes	14	36	21	9
Non-priests lead some parishes	15	3	21	9
Increase retirement age	6	3	3	17

*Differences between each type of responding bishop are statistically significant.
Source: CARA Survey of Bishops, 2016.

Table C6.2 Comparison of Different Types of Bishops on Willingness to Use Different Types of Personnel to Lead Parishes in the Absence of a Priest

Responded "Very Willing"	Active Latin Rite Ordinary (%)	Latin Rite Auxiliary (%)	Retired Latin Rite (%)	Eastern Rite (%)
Permanent deacon	63	57	59	58
Religious sister*	31	10	39	9
Religious brother*	30	13	33	9
Lay woman*	26	3	29	9
Lay man	25	0	29	9

*Differences between each type of responding bishop are statistically significant.
Source: CARA Survey of Bishops, 2016.

Table C6.3 Comparing Different Types of Bishops on Scope of Policies

Detailed/Highly Standardized Policies	Active Latin Rite Ordinary (%)	Latin Rite Auxiliary (%)	Retired Latin Rite (%)	Eastern Rite (%)
Liturgy*	13	29	22	50
Sacramental preparation*	18	29	37	27
Finances	50	58	57	25
Personnel*	32	48	32	0
Religious education*	18	42	33	17

*Differences between each type of responding bishop are statistically significant.
Source: CARA Survey of Bishops, 2016.

Appendix C

Chapter 7: The Bishops Speak

Table C7.1 Comparing Different Types of Bishops on Topics They Write On

Write on Topic on a Regular Basis	Active Latin Rite Ordinary (%)	Latin Rite Auxiliary (%)	Retired Latin Rite (%)	Eastern Rite (%)
Catholic teaching on sanctity of life*	38	8	39	17
Spiritual or biblical reflection*	34	16	38	25
Catholic theology*	33	12	29	33
Catholic teaching on the family*	26	8	25	17
Catholic social teaching*	24	12	29	0
Religious freedom issues*	22	13	11	8
Catholic teaching on sexual morality*	15	8	19	0

*Differences between each type of responding bishop are statistically significant.
Source: CARA Survey of Bishops, 2016.

Table C7.2 Comparing Different Types of Bishops on Political Activity.

Political Action on a Regular Basis	Active Latin Rite Ordinary (%)	Latin Rite Auxiliary (%)	Retired Latin Rite (%)	Eastern Rite (%)
Asked Catholics to consider Catholic teaching when voting for candidates	37	28	26	17
Lobbied lawmakers or other political leaders about current social issues*	24	10	9	0
Made statements to the general public about social or political issues*	21	11	10	0
Asked Catholics to vote a particular way on a ballot initiative or referendum	1	0	0	0

*Differences between each type of responding bishop are statistically significant.
Source: CARA Survey of Bishops, 2016.

Table C7.3 Comparing Different Types of Bishops on Media Experience

Views on Media	Active Latin Rite Ordinary (%)	Latin Rite Auxiliary (%)	Retired Latin Rite (%)	Eastern Rite (%)
Media coverage of clergy sexual abuse has made it challenging to present or defend Church teaching in my diocese—*Agree strongly*	21	42	35	18
How much media coverage (local/national) directed at your current diocese in the wake of the revelations of clergy sexual abuse—*Extensive coverage**	18	44	18	0
Criticism in secular press or media on a day to day basis is—*A great problem*	18	49	28	25

*Differences between each type of responding bishop are statistically significant.
Source: CARA Survey of Bishops, 2016.

References

Allen, John. "'Baby Bishops' Get a Crash Course in the Realities of the Church." *Crux*, September 18, 2016. https://cruxnow.com/vatican/2016/09/18/baby-bishops-get-crash-course-realities-church/.

Allen, John. "With Pope's Cardinal Picks, Bernardin's 'Seamless Garment' is Back." *Crux*, October 9, 2016. https://cruxnow.com/analysis/2016/10/09/popes-cardinal-picks-bernardins-seamless-garment-back/.

Aviv, Rachel. "Revenge Killing: Race and the Death Penalty in a Louisiana Parish." *The New Yorker*, July 6 and 13, 2015. http://www.newyorker.com/magazine/2015/07/06/revenge-killing.

Brunson, Matthew. "Recap of USCCB Assembly Day 2: Debating Faithful Citizenship." *Our Sunday Visitor Weekly*, November 18, 2015. https://www.osv.com/OSVNewsweekly/Article/TabId/535/ArtMID/13567/ArticleID/18734/Recap-of-USCCB-assembly-Day-2-Debating-faithful-citizenship.aspx.

Bureau of Labor Statistics, U.S. Department of Labor. *American Time Use Survey*, 2017. https://www.bls.gov/tus/.

Burke, Daniel. "Catholic Bishops Denounce Film on Clerical Celibacy; Moviemaker Says HBO Documentary Aims to Go Beyond Headlines on Church Sex-Abuse Scandal." *Washington Post*, June 26, 2014, B7.

Carroll, Jackson W. *God's Potters: Pastoral Leadership and the Shaping of Congregations*. Grand Rapids, MI: William B. Eerdmans, 2006.

Catechism of the Catholic Church. New York: Doubleday, 1995.

Catholic Democrats and Catholics in Alliance for the Common Good. Untitled letter to the candidates for president of the US Conference of Catholic Bishops (USCCB), 2013. http://catholicdemocrats.org/BishopLetter.pdf.

Center for Applied Research in the Apostolate. CARA Catholic Poll September 2012 [Data file]. Washington, DC: Center for Applied Research in the Apostolate, 2012.

Center for Applied Research in the Apostolate. CARA Catholic Poll September 2015 [Data file]. Washington, DC: Center for Applied Research in the Apostolate, 2015.

Center for Applied Research in the Apostolate. "Lay Ecclesial Ministers in the United States." Presentation at United States Conference of Catholic Bishops Lay Ecclesial Ministry Summit. St. Louis, MO, July 7, 2015.

Center for Applied Research in the Apostolate. CARA Survey of Bishops [Data file]. Washington, DC: Center for Applied Research in the Apostolate, 2016.

Cheney, David M. Catholic-Hierarchy, 2017. http://www.catholic-hierarchy.org/country/us.html.

Duckett, Richard. "Bishop Attacks Question 2; Ballot Initiative 'Morally Flawed.'" *Sunday Telegram* (Massachusetts), October 28, 2012, B1.

Du Saussay, André. *Panoplia Episcopalis.* Paris, 1646, 175–294.

D'Zurilla, Christie. "Kate Beckinsale: Harvey Weinstein 'Is an Emblem of a System that Is Sick.'" October 12, 2017. http://www.latimes.com/entertainment/la-et-entertainment-news-updates-kate-beckinsale-harvey-1507827299-htmlstory.html.

Favot, Sarah. "Lowell-Area Catholics Hear Bishop Decry Assisted Suicide." *Lowell Sun*, February 13, 2012.

Fichter, Joseph H. *America's Forgotten Priests: What They are Saying.* New York: Harper & Row, 1968.

Gaunt, Thomas P. Bishop Demographic and Educational Information from Diocesan Websites [Data file]. Washington, DC: Center for Applied Research in the Apostolate, 2016.

Gautier, Mary L. "Did You Know? Female Chancellors." *Nineteen Sixty-four* (blog), Center for Applied Research in the Apostolate, August 25, 2016. http://nineteensixty-four.blogspot.com/2016/08/did-you-know-female-chancellors.html.

Gautier, Mary L., Melissa A. Cidade, Paul M. Perl, and Mark M. Gray. *Bridging the Gap: The Opportunities and Challenges of International Priests Ministering in the United States.* Huntington, IN: Our Sunday Visitor Inc., 2014.

Gautier, Mary L., Paul M. Perl, and Stephen J. Fichter. *Same Call, Different Men: The Evolution of the Priesthood since Vatican II.* Collegeville, MN: Liturgical Press, 2012.

Gautier, Mary L., Tricia C. Bruce, and Mary E. Bendyna. *Listening to the Spirit: Bishops and Parish Life Coordinators.* Washington, DC: Center for Applied Research in the Apostolate, 2007.

Gray, Mark M. "Coming Home." *Nineteen Sixty-four* (blog), Center for Applied Research in the Apostolate, April 22, 2011. http://nineteensixty-four.blogspot.com/2011/04/coming-home.html.

Gray, Mark M., and Paul M. Perl. *Catholic Reactions to the News of Sexual Abuse Cases Involving Catholic Clergy.* Washington, DC: Center for Applied Research in the Apostolate, 2006. http://cara.georgetown.edu/Publications/workingpapers/CARAWorkingPaper8.pdf.

Greeley, Andrew M. *Priests: A Calling Crisis.* Chicago: University of Chicago Press, 2004.

Heimlich, Russell. "Most U.S. Catholics Say They are Satisfied with the Leadership Provided by U.S. Nuns and Sisters." Washington, DC: Pew Research Center, August, 6, 2012. http://www.pewresearch.org/fact-tank/2012/08/06/most-u-s-catholics-say-they-are-satisfied-with-the-leadership-provided-by-u-s-nuns-and-sisters/.

Hirshkowitz, Max, Kaitlyn Whiton, Steven M. Albert, Cathy Alessi, Oliviero Bruni, Lydia DonCarlos . . . Paula J. Adams Hillard. "National Sleep Foundation's Sleep Time Duration Recommendations: Methodology and Results Summary," *Sleep Health* 1, no. 1 (2015). http://www.sleephealthjournal.org/article/S2352-7218%2815%2900015-7/fulltext.

Hoegeman, Catherine. Bishop Information Database, 1978–2017. [Datafile]. Springfield, MO: Missouri State University, 2017.

Hoge, Dean R., and Jacqueline E. Wenger. *Evolving Visions of the Priesthood: Changes from Vatican II to the Turn of the New Century.* Collegeville, MN: Liturgical Press, 2003.

Kilpatrick, James. "Bishops Could Take a Tip from Burke." *Detroit Free Press,* November 20, 1986, 9.

Kramarek, Michal J., and Thomas P. Gaunt. *National Diocesan Survey: Salary and Benefits for Priests and Lay Personnel 2017.* Washington DC: National Association of Church Personnel Administrators, 2017.

Lipka, Michael, and Benjamin Wormald. "How Religious is Your State?" Pew Research Center, February 29, 2016. http://www.pewresearch.org/fact-tank/2016/02/29/how-religious-is-your-state/.

Malone, Richard J. "USCCB Lay Ecclesial Ministry Summit Report." Presentation at United States Conference of Catholic Bishops Lay Ecclesial Ministry Summit. St. Louis, MO, 2015.

McElwee, Joshua J. "Groups Urge US Bishops to Speak on Poverty, Build 'Church for the Poor.'" *National Catholic Reporter,* November 11, 2013. https://www.ncronline.org/blogs/ncr-today/groups-urge-us-bishops-speak-poverty-build-church-poor.

Mogilka, Mark, and Kate Wiskus. *Pastoring Multiple Parishes.* Chicago: Loyola Press, 2009.

Mohler, Albert. "Getting American Religion: A Conversation with Former *Newsweek* Religion Editor Kenneth L. Woodward." December 5, 2016. http://www.albertmohler.com/2016/12/05/getting-american-religion/.

National Review Board for the Protection of Children and Young People. *A Report on the Crisis in the Catholic Church in the United States.* Washington, DC: USCCB, 2004. http://www.usccb.org/issues-and-action/child-and-youth-protection/upload/a-report-on-the-crisis-in-the-catholic-church-in-the-united-states-by-the-national-review-board.pdf.

Norman, Jim. "Americans Rate Healthcare Providers High on Honesty, Ethics." *Gallup,* December 19, 2016. http://www.gallup.com/poll/200057/americans-rate-healthcare-providers-high-honesty-ethics.aspx.

Pew Research Center Forum on Religion & Public Life. "The Catholic 'Swing' Vote." October 11, 2012. http://www.pewforum.org/2012/10/11/the-catholic-swing-vote/.

Pew Research Center U.S. Politics & Policy. "In Changing News Landscape, Even Television is Vulnerable: Trends in News Consumption: 1991–2012." September 27, 2012. http://www.people-press.org/2012/09/27/in-changing-news-landscape-|even-television-is-vulnerable/.

Pope Francis. *Apostolic Exhortation Evangelii Gaudium*, November 24, 2013. https://w2.vatican.va/content/francesco/en/apost_exhortations/documents/papa-francesco_esortazione-ap_20131124_evangelii-gaudium.html.

Reese, Thomas J. *Archbishop: Inside the Power Structure of the American Catholic Church*. New York: Harper & Row, 1989.

Rice, Patricia. "Catholics Hope Policy Will Revive Church's Moral Clout." *St. Louis Post-Dispatch*, November 24, 2002, B1.

Roberts, Tom. "At USCCB Meeting, Bishops Slow to Adopt Pope's Vision." *National Catholic Reporter*, December 1, 2015. https://www.ncronline.org/news/vatican/parsing-priorities-and-plans-meeting-bishops-slow-adopt-popes-vision.

Roberts, Tom. "Bishops Pass 'Faithful Citizenship,' Some Call for New Document." *National Catholic Reporter*, November 17, 2015. https://www.ncronline.org/news/vatican/us-bishops-pass-revised-faithful-citizenship-some-call-new-document.

Rossetti, Stephen. *Why Priests Are Happy: A Study of the Psychological and Spiritual Health of Priests*. Notre Dame, IN: Ave Maria Press, 2011.

Rossetti, Stephen J., and Colin J. Rhoades. "Burnout in Catholic Clergy: A Predictive Model Using Psychological and Spiritual Variables," *Psychology of Religion and Spirituality* 5, no. 4 (2013): 335–341.

Second Vatican Council. *The Dogmatic Constitution on the Church: Lumen Gentium*, November 21, 1964. http://www.vatican.va/archive/hist_councils/ii_vatican_council/documents/vat-ii_const_19641121_lumen-gentium_en.html.

Second Vatican Council. *Decree Concerning the Pastoral Office of the Bishops in the Church: Christus Dominus*, October 28, 1965. http://www.vatican.va/archive/hist_councils/ii_vatican_council/documents/vat-ii_decree_19651028_christus-dominus_en.html.

Second Vatican Council. *Decree on the Up-to-Date Renewal of Religious Life: Perfectae Caritatis*, October 28, 1965. http://www.vatican.va/archive/hist_councils/ii_vatican_council/documents/vat-ii_decree_19651028_perfectae-caritatis_en.html.

Second Vatican Council. *Decree on the Apostolate of the Laity: Apostolicam Actusoitatem*, November 18, 1965. http://www.vatican.va/archive/hist_councils/ii_vatican_council/documents/vat-ii_decree_19651118_apostolicam-actuositatem_en.html.

Second Vatican Council. *Pastoral Constitution on the Church in the Modern World, Gaudium et Spes*, December 7, 1965. http://www.vatican.va/archive/hist_councils/ii_vatican_council/documents/vat-ii_cons_19651207_gaudium-et-spes_en.html.

Smith, Tom W., Peter Marsden, Michael Hout, and Jibum Kim. General Social Surveys, 1972–2016 [Data file]. Chicago: NORC at the University of Chicago, 2016.

Snider, Mike. "Cable News Ratings Drop Post-Election." *USA Today*, February 1, 2017. https://www.pressreader.com/usa/usa-today-us-edition/20170201/281556585554558.

Stark, Rodney, and Roger Finke. "Catholic Religious Vocations: Decline and Renewal," *Review of Religious Research* 45, no. 2 (2000): 125–145.

Synod of Bishops. XIII Ordinary General Assembly, *The New Evangelization for the Transmission of the Christian Faith.* Instrumentum Laboris, Vatican City, 2012.

The Canon Law Society of America. *Code of Canon Law.* Washington, DC: Liberia Editrice Vaticana, 2003. http://www.vatican.va/archive/ENG1104/_INDEX. HTM.

The Official Catholic Directory. New Providence, NJ: P.J. Kenedy & Sons, 1985–2016.

United States Conference of Catholic Bishops. *Economic Justice for All: Pastoral Letter on Catholic Social Teaching and the U.S. Economy.* Washington, DC: USCCB, 1986.

United States Conference of Catholic Bishops. *Strengthening the Bonds of Peace*, November 1994. http://www.usccb.org/about/laity-marriage-family-life-and-youth/womens-issues/strengthening-the-bonds-of-peace.cfm.

United States Conference of Catholic Bishops. *From Words to Deeds: Continuing Reflections on the Role of Women in the Church*, September 15, 1998. http://www.usccb.org/about/laity-marriage-family-life-and-youth/womens-issues/from-words-to-deeds.cfm.

United States Conference of Catholic Bishops. *Welcoming the Stranger Among Us: Unity in Diversity*, November 15, 2000. http://www.usccb.org/issues-and-action/cultural-diversity/pastoral-care-of-migrants-refugees-and-travelers/re-sources/welcoming-the-stranger-among-us-unity-in-diversity.cfm.

United States Conference of Catholic Bishops. *A Place at the Table: A Catholic Recommitment to Overcome Poverty and to Respect the Dignity of All God's Children*, November 13, 2002. http://www.usccb.org/issues-and-action/human-life-and-dignity/poverty/place-at-the-table.cfm.

United States Conference of Catholic Bishops. *Co-Workers in the Vineyard of the Lord.* Washington, DC: USCCB, 2005. http://www.usccb.org/laity/laymin/co-workers.pdf.

United States Conference of Catholic Bishops. *Essential Norms for Diocesan/Eparchial Policies Dealing with Allegations of Sexual Abuse of Minors by Priests or Deacons.* Washington, DC: USCCB, 2006. http://www.usccb.org/issues-and-action/child-and-youth-protection/upload/Charter-for-the-Protection-of-Children-and-Young-People-revised-2011.pdf

United States Conference of Catholic Bishops. *Guidelines for Receiving Pastoral Ministers in the United States.* Third Edition. Washington, DC: USCCB, 2014.

United States Conference of Catholic Bishops. "The Defense of Marriage and Right of Religious Freedom Open Letter 2015," April 23, 2015. http://www.usccb.org/issues-and-action/marriage-and-family/marriage/promotion-and-defense-of-marriage/defense-of-marriage-and-right-of-religious-freedom-open-letter-2015.cfm.

United States Conference of Catholic Bishops. *Forming Consciences for Faithful Citizenship: A Call to Political Responsibility from the Catholic Bishops of the United States with Introductory Note.* Washington, DC: USCCB, 2015. http://www.usccb.org/issues-and-action/faithful-citizenship/forming-consciences-for-faithful-citizenship-title.cfm.

United States Conference of Catholic Bishops. *About USCCB,* July 9, 2017. http://www.usccb.org/about/.

United States Conference of Catholic Bishops. *Charter for the Protection of Children and Young People.* Washington, DC: USCCB, 2018. http://www.usccb.org/issues-and-action/child-and-youth-protection/upload/Charter-for-the-Protection-of-Children-and-Young-People-2018.pdf.

University of Chicago News Office. "Looking for Satisfaction and Happiness in a Career? Start by Choosing a Job that Helps Others." April 17, 2007. http://www-news.uchicago.edu/releases/07/070417.jobs.shtml.

U.S. Bureau of the Census. International Data Base [Data file]. Washington, DC: U.S. Bureau of the Census, 2015.

Wakin, Daniel J. "Refusing to Recant, Keating Resigns as Church Panel Chief." *New York Times,* June 17, 2003. http://www.nytimes.com/2003/06/17/us/refusing-to-recant-keating-resigns-as-church-panel-chief.html.

Wiess, Debra Cassens. "Law is Second-Most Sleep-Deprived Profession, Federal Survey Finds," *ABA Journal,* February 27, 2012. http://www.abajournal.com/news/article/law_is_second-most_sleep_deprived_profession_federal_survey_finds/.

Winters, Michael Sean. "The Dallas Charter is on Life-Support." *The National Catholic Reporter,* June 2, 2011. https://www.ncronline.org/blogs/distinctly-catholic/dallas-charter-life-support.

Zapor, Patricia. "Voters in Three States Approve Laws Permitting Same Sex Marriage." *Catholic News Service,* November 9, 2012. http://www.catholicnews.com/services/englishnews/2012/voters-in-three-states-approve-laws-permitting-same-sex-marriage-cns-1204732.cfm.

Zech, Charles E., Mary L. Gautier, Mark M. Gray, Jonathon L. Wiggins, and Thomas P. Gaunt. *Catholic Parishes of the 21st Century.* New York, NY: Oxford University Press, 2017.

Index